Workers' Handbooks

Maurice Frankel Social Audit

CHEMICAL RISK

A Workers' Guide to Chemical Hazards and Data Sheets

Pluto  Press

This edition first published 1982 in
Great Britain by Pluto Press Limited,
Unit 10, Spencer Court, 7 Chalcot Road,
London NW1 8LH

Copyright © Social Audit 1982

ISBN 0 86104 362 6

Cover design by Colin Bailey

Typeset by Wayside Graphics,
Clevedon, Avon
Printed in Great Britain by Photobooks
(Bristol) Limited, Barton Manor,
St Philips, Bristol BS2 0RN

Contents

Preface

In 1981 Social Audit published a report examining the health and safety information provided by chemical suppliers to the users of their products. (Maurice Frankel, *A Word of Warning: The Quality of Suppliers' Health and Safety Information*, £7.95.) People at work rely on such information for their safety – yet much of it was found to be seriously inadequate.

Chemical Risk is also based on this research. It is intended to help workers, and in particular trade union representatives, deal with the problems caused by chemicals – and by poor information. However, it also discusses the information policies of chemical suppliers and employers and so may be of wider interest.

Chemical Risk was prepared at Social Audit, an independent non profit-making organisation concerned with improving government and corporate accountability. Social Audit is also the publishing arm of Public Interest Research Centre, a charity which conducts research into government and corporate activities and which carried out the research on which this book is based.

The research for this book was funded by a grant from the Social Science Research Council. We gratefully acknowledge this assistance and the continued support of the Joseph Rowntree Charitable Trust and the Joseph Rowntree Social Service Trust. In addition, I would like to thank my colleagues Virginia Beardshaw, Barbara Freese and Charles Medawar for their considerable help and Dave Gee and Sheila McKechnie for much excellent advice.

Maurice Frankel   Social Audit
September 1981   9 Poland Street, London W1V 3DG

1 Introduction

'One of the real pitfalls of giving information to safety representatives, or to anybody working on the shop floor, is to convey the impression of giving what one thinks the enquirer ought to have, and not the whole truth.

'I suspect that in an educated democracy people are entitled to have the lot. I suspect that the safety representative will make as good a judgement about it as anyone else. They will make a very poor judgement if they feel that some of the facts are being withheld.' Bryan Harvey, chairman of the Health and Safety Commission's Advisory Committee on Major Hazards and former Chief Inspector of Factories in a talk given 17 February 1979.

The Health and Safety at Work Act

The 1974 Health and Safety at Work Act brought two major changes in the control of workplace hazards:

It allowed recognised trade unions at any workplace to appoint safety representatives from the workforce. Safety representatives are legally entitled to carry out safety inspections in the workplace; to investigate accidents, potential hazards and complaints from employees; and to make representations to their employer on such matters.

The Act also created a series of disclosure of information duties. The manufacturer or supplier of any article or substance used at work must make health and safety information on the product available to the user. The employer must make this – and any other relevant information – available to safety representatives.

Suppliers' data sheets

Chemical suppliers normally provide health and safety information in the form of data sheets – though it may also be provided in letters, on wallcharts or in instruction manuals. (For the sake of convenience, the term 'suppliers' data sheets' is used to cover all of these throughout this book.)

Suppliers' data sheets are only one of a variety of sources of information on chemical hazards that should be available to users. But it may be the only source that is:

- *Easily accessible* – the alternatives may be expensive reference books or obscure, and difficult to understand, scientific periodicals.
- *Comprehensive* – information in the published sources may be scattered amongst a variety of publications, each specialising in a different area. A good data sheet will gather all this information together.
- *Available at all* – although manufacturers must test their products, they are not obliged to publish their findings. In some cases there may be no published information on a chemical – other than the data sheet.

For these reasons safety representatives – and in many cases employers – may use suppliers' data sheets as their main source of information on chemical hazards. In many establishments, the health of the workforce may well depend on the quality of this information.

A safety representative may typically turn to the data sheets if he or she finds that employees in a certain part of the workplace are complaining about chemical fumes, or suffering from an unusual amount of illness. The safety representative may want to know what chemicals are used in the products they handle, what their hazards are, what safety measures should be used – and whether existing precautions are adequate, or need improving.

A good data sheet will give all this information, and more. But many data sheets fall far short of what is needed.

A senior American official has described the problems of data sheets in the USA – and the comment applies equally in the UK:

'The quality of manufacturers' data sheets is very variable. Those manufacturers with both the resources and desire to do a complete and frank analysis do so. Although a number of manufacturers fall into this category, *many of them lack either the necessary resources, will or both.*' Frank W. Mackison, US National Institute of Occupational Safety and Health in a letter to Social Audit, 14 May 1980.

About this book

This book illustrates some of the best – and some of the worst – features of suppliers' information in the UK. It includes some fifty examples taken either from data sheets in circulation between 1978 and 1980 or from interviews with suppliers during this period. Some of these examples draw attention to the characteristic weaknesses of some data sheets; others illustrate that a high standard of information is possible – and should be insisted on.

This book describes the information safety representatives should be given about chemicals used in the workplace – and explains how this information can be interpreted and used. It explains:

- Safety representatives' rights to information, and what they can do if information is refused.
- Why it is essential to know the chemical composition of products – and how safety representatives can deal with the problem of unidentified 'trade-name' products.
- What information safety representatives need about the hazards of chemicals and the handling of emergencies – and what problems they may face from arbitrary judgements and untested chemicals.
- The basic methods of controlling hazards, and the use and abuse of 'TLV' exposure limits.
- How data sheets should be used – and what can be done to detect and deal with unreliable data sheets.
- What information policies should be adopted by employers.
- How to use published sources of information to investigate chemical hazards.

Finally, a standard data sheet is given. It incorporates many of the best features of existing data sheets, and other features which are completely new. Its aim is to help safety representatives recognise inadequate data sheets and to provide a ready-made alternative which suppliers or employers can be asked to complete.

2 Your right to information

Although the hazards of chemicals may be described in a variety of published sources, these can be difficult to get hold of. Not only safety representatives but even employers may have considerable trouble in finding this information.

The Health and Safety at Work Act (HSWA) recognised this and has tried to ensure that all users of chemicals at work can obtain health and safety information from their suppliers.

The basic legal duties are described in full on page 91. In summary, they require that:

The **manufacturer** of any substance used at work must carry out research to discover and minimise its hazards. (HSWA, section 6(5).)

The **supplier** of any substance used at work must ensure that adequate health and safety information is available to users. (HSWA, section 6(4)(c).) Certain substances must also be labelled with their names and with prescribed hazard symbols and phrases. (Packaging and Labelling of Dangerous Substances Regulations 1978)

The **employer** must give employees any information necessary to protect their health and safety at work. (HSWA, section 2(2)(c).)

The **employer** must make available to safety representatives any information she or he has that they need in order to carry out their functions, including any information received from suppliers. (Regulations on Safety Representatives and Safety Committees 1977)

The **factory inspector** should enforce these requirements and must also help to keep employees informed about any hazards at work and about any action that she or he takes. (HSWA Section 28(8).)

Suppliers' data sheets

If these arrangements work properly:

- *suppliers* should make health and safety information on their products available to *users,* and
- *employers* should make any suppliers' information they obtain available to *safety representatives.*

Suppliers' information is usually provided on data sheets. These data sheets are the one source of information that should be readily available both to your employer and to you. It is essential that this information should be accurate and complete.

This chapter tells you exactly what information on the hazards of a product you should be getting from suppliers.

The supplier's legal obligations

'It shall be the duty of any person who manufactures, imports or supplies any substance for use at work . . . to take such steps as are necessary to secure that there will be available in connection with the use of the substance at work adequate information about the results of any relevant tests which have been carried out on or in connection with the substance and about any conditions necessary to ensure that it will be safe and without risks to health when properly used.' (Health and Safety at Work Act, section 6(4)(c).)

If you read this passage carefully you will see that suppliers must provide users with *two* kinds of information:

1. the *hazards* of the product ('. . . the results of any relevant tests . . .') and

2. the necessary *safety precautions.*

The Health and Safety Commission has produced a Guidance Note on the duties of suppliers. The Guidance Note emphasises that suppliers must provide *specific* information on their products' hazards:

'It is not sufficient (for the supplier) merely to draw the attention of the user to the dangerous nature of the substance. Reference should also be made to *the specific nature of the hazards* . . .' 'Articles and Substances for Use at Work'. Health and Safety Commission, Guidance Note GS/8.

The Guidance Note adds that the supplier should:

'ensure that the user is aware of the *risks* to which the substance may give rise, the *circumstances* in which such risks may be accentuated, and the *means* whereby they may be reduced to a level which does not jeopardise the safety and health of the user's employees'. (italics added)

The other relevant parts of the Guidance Note are reproduced on pages 93–5.

One of the Health and Safety Executive's senior chemical inspectors has added this explanation of the supplier's duties:

'Section 6 says "adequate information". The information is only adequate when it explains the information fairly thoroughly and is within the understanding of the person to whom it has been given. *If he is not satisfied by the information then it is not adequate.*' A. G. Wilkie, speaking at a conference of 'Hazards and Control of Toxic Substances in the Manufacturing Industries', 17 February 1979.

Summarising these points, we can see that the suppliers are required to:

1. Describe the *specific hazards* of the product. A general warning that the product is dangerous is not enough.

2. Describe the *conditions likely to be dangerous* for example, the concentration or period of exposure known to cause injury.
3. Describe the *necessary safety precautions*.
4. Provide *all the information needed* by the user, in a way the user can understand.

3 Identifying the chemicals

The precautions needed to handle chemicals safely vary from substance to substance. So the first step in controlling chemical hazards is always to identify the chemicals used in the workplace.

Unfortunately, many chemical products are sold under trade-names – manufacturers keep the actual composition secret. It may be difficult for workers – and even for employers – to discover the names of the chemicals used in these products. Without this information, users can never be certain that they understand the hazards they face and have taken all the necessary safety precautions.

Some idea of the size of the problem can be seen from a 1974 US government survey. The survey found that 95,000 different trade-named products were used by the firms questioned. The composition of 90 per cent of these products was totally unknown to the companies using them. Some of the products contained substances known to cause cancer in humans. But the customers – and their workforces – had not been told of the risk because the manufacturers refused to identify the ingredients.

This chapter explains precisely why workers need to know the names of the chemicals they use, and how this information can be obtained.

Why trade-names are used

Instead of describing the chemical composition of a product, trade-names will often refer to the name of the manufacturer ('Shellsol', 'Solvesso', 'Dowper') or to the job that the product does ('Styccobond F61', 'SN 1337 Carton Grade Dry Spray Powder').

A trade-name may be used because:

- The product contains a mixture of many different chemicals, so a single name is convenient and easy to remember.
- It helps to distinguish the product from competing products, and encourages the customer to keep buying from the same manufacturer.
- It conceals the real identity of the product. This may be done to prevent competitors duplicating the product. But often the composition is well known to competitors who produce virtually identical products themselves. If customers realised this, they would shop around until they found the cheapest buy. The manufacturer will often try to keep the composition secret from customers simply to stop them buying the same product elsewhere.

Why you need to know the chemical composition

There are four main reasons why users must know the chemical composition of trade-name products they handle:

- **to choose the least toxic product capable of doing the job**
- **to adopt proper control measures**
- **to be able to give proper medical treatment in cases of poisoning**
- **to be able to check independently the accuracy of suppliers' health and safety information.**

Choose the least toxic product capable of doing the job

Whenever hazardous substances are used, users should try to avoid the risk by substituting less toxic alternatives. Substitution is standard practice for dealing with certain highly toxic substances such as asbestos, benzene, trichloroethylene and toluene di-isocyanate (but it is important to realise that the alternatives to these products are not completely safe – and in fact have their own toxic properties. See *Example 1.*) It is impossible to compare the hazards of unidentified trade-named products: the chemical composition of the alternatives must be known. See *Example 2.*

Select proper control measures

Users need to know the composition of trade-named products in order to:

● *Example 1.* **Replacing the product may reduce, but not eliminate, the hazard**

In one workplace trichloroethane was substituted for the more toxic trichloroethylene. A radiator and metal tank repairer was involved in an aircraft tip tank cleaning and assembly operation . . . One particular worker would saturate a pad with solvent and lower himself head first into a tank that needed cleaning and clean as fast as possible. This worker was found with his legs protruding from the upper end of the 450 gallon tank and was unresponsive. He was removed immediately and was given artificial respiration until a physician arrived and pronounced him dead.

'Reconstruction of the fatal accident revealed the concentration of trichloroethane in the tank had reached 62,000 ppm. *The workers assumed that since the new cleaning solvent was less toxic than the one previously used, there was less danger.*' US National Institute for Occupational Safety and Health, 'Working in Confined Spaces, Criteria for a Recommended Standard', 1979.

● *Example 2.* **Substitution**

'**The use of benzene should be abandoned for any industrial purpose where an effective, less harmful substitute is available.**' International Labour Office, *Encyclopaedia of Occupational Health and Safety*, 1972.

The composition of two alternative products is shown below. Both are paint strippers, manufactured by the same company.

'KLEAN KUTTER' Acetone, Benzene, Methanol.

'KLEAN STRIP FORMULA A' Aluminium hydroxide, Isopropyl alcohol, Methylene chloride, Propylene dichloride.

For certain jobs, either of these products might be effective. **But only if users know the composition of both can they choose the less dangerous – the benzene-free – product.** Note that this does not mean that the alternative is safe: its ingredients also have toxic properties.

● **ensure that ventilation is adequate**
● **monitor contamination levels in the air, and**
● **select the right protective equipment.**

Ventilation

Data sheets on trade-named products frequently recommend that 'adequate' or 'good' ventilation should be used, without specifying precisely what standard of ventilation should be

Example 3. **Standards of ventilation**

Four extracts from suppliers' data sheets are shown below. Only the last properly defines the standard of ventilation required.

1. '*Good ventilation* is an essential when R.I.W. 606 Hardener is being used, as it gives off an irritant vapour.'
2. 'Avoid breathing the vapour of Propocons, which should always be used in a *well-ventilated* area.'
3. 'Nalfloc N158-D is a viscous organic liquid containing dispersants, stabilisers and corrosion inhibitors . . . Avoid prolonged or repeated breathing of the vapour. Ensure *adequate ventilation.*'
4. 'It is recommended that the . . . average atmospheric concentration for continuous working conditions during a normal working day does not exceed 50 ppm (TLV)* . . . Adequate ventilation should be provided . . . Ethylene oxide should NOT be used in confined or badly ventilated spaces. Working areas in which the atmosphere is suspected to contain vapour, particularly in enclosed buildings, should be regularly monitored. Where more than 50 ppm is found *immediate* attention must be given to the source of leakage and the dispersal of the vapour or liquid.'

*Note: 'TLV' stands for 'Threshold Limit Value' – standards limiting the concentrations of dusts or gases allowed in the workroom air. They are described more fully on page 51. The TLV for ethylene oxide was reduced from 50 ppm to 10 ppm in 1981.

involved. The first three extracts in *Example 3* all refer to unidentified trade-named products, and all fail to specify the level of ventilation needed.

These examples assume that 'good' ventilation is a single condition that applies to all substances. In fact, ventilation that may adequately control a particular substance may be quite inadequate against other more toxic substances, or against substances which evaporate into the air more quickly.

To know precisely what 'adequate ventilation' involves, you must know (1) the name of the substance, and (2) the concentration of the substance in the air that the ventilation must be capable of achieving. Note how this has been done in the last extract in *Example 3*.

Monitoring

The last extract in *Example 3* stresses that *monitoring is essential* to check that contamination levels in the air are kept low. This is in line with the Health and Safety Executive's advice that:

'Where the atmosphere of a workplace is likely to be contaminated, sampling of the atmosphere and subsequent analysis should be carried out on a periodic basis.' Guidance Note EH/15.

Monitoring methods vary depending on the substance involved: to measure the level of a substance in the air you must know which substance it is that you are dealing with. Some data sheets may recommend that an air quality standard such as a TLV (see page 51) be met, without identifying the chemical to which it applies:

'Ardrox 26 HT contains a tar acid which has a TLV of 5 ppm.'

'Volatile solvents . . . Occupational exposure standard 500 ppm.'

This advice cannot be followed, because it is impossible to measure the concentration of an unidentified vapour.

Protective equipment
The names of chemicals being handled must also be known in order to choose the right protective equipment:

'In addition to the toxicity and expected concentration of the contaminant, both the physical form and the identity of the contaminant must be known so that the proper respirator can be selected.' N. I. Sax, *Dangerous Properties of Industrial Materials*, 5th edition 1979.

'Respirators for gases . . . should be used only against those gases specifically indicated on the cannister or cartridge.' British Standards Institution, *Recommendations for the selection, use and maintenance of respiratory protective equipment*, BS 4275:1974.

Protective gloves or other clothing must be made of materials known to be resistant to the chemicals being used. See *Example 4*.

Poisoning

A standard reference book on the treatment of poisoning states:

'If a patient has been exposed to a substance whose ingredients are not known, the physician must identify the contents without delay. This problem is complicated by the great numbers of trade-named mixtures and the rapidity with which the formulas for such mixtures change. Since most trade-named chemical mixtures do not list the ingredients on the label, it is usually not possible to evaluate the significance of contact with such materials without further information.' R. H. Dreisbach, *Handbook of Poisoning*, Lange Medical Publications, 1974.

● *Example 4.* **Protective clothing**

The materials used for protective clothing are not equally resistant to all chemicals. The table below shows the length of time that clothing made of neoprene rubber (0.76 mm thick) kept different chemicals off the skin.

Substance	Protection time
Coal-tar creosote	$4\frac{1}{2}$ hours
Epichlorohydrin	60–80 minutes
Benzene	25 minutes
Trichloroethylene	10–15 minutes

Source: US National Institute for Occupational Safety and Health. 'Development of Performance Criteria for Protective Clothing Used Against Carcinogenic Liquids', October 1978.

If a person has been overcome by unidentified chemical fumes there may be crucial delays before a doctor can decide on the correct treatment. See *Example 5.*

In a life-or-death emergency, chemical suppliers will reveal normally secret information to a doctor. But it may not always be possible to contact the supplier immediately because telephones may be unattended at nights or weekends. Even if they can be contacted, some suppliers may not be able to help. They may have made their products by blending *other* trade-named substances together: they may not be able to give the doctor the full chemical composition because they don't actually know it themselves. See *Example 6.*

There are other emergency sources of information about trade-named products that can be used by doctors in an emergency. Both the Health and Safety Executive and a number of Poisons Centres at selected hospitals in the UK have files of information on the composition of some trade-named products. But these files do not cover *all* trade-named products.

If the chemicals in a product are not identified on the container label or on a data sheet, a doctor may be unable to get this information from any other source in an emergency – and a patient's life may be at risk as a result.

Compensation
The use of unidentified trade-named products may also prevent workers who develop occupational diseases from obtaining

Example 5. **The treatment of poisoning** (see point 3)

Emergency Procedures...

 TIME IS THE MOST IMPORTANT FACTOR!!

Know the following before an accident occurs:

1. Know where emergency equipment is located.
2. Know phone number and location of medical help.
3. Be able to tell medical help the specific name of chemical causing the injury.
4. Know the emergency procedures described below.

Source: US National Institute for Occupational Safety and Health, 'Caution: Inorganic Metal Cleaners Can Be Dangerous', Publication No. 76–110.

compensation. To get compensation, a worker must be able to prove which chemicals caused the illness – and this may be impossible if trade-named products were involved.

Check the suppliers' information

Not all suppliers are able to provide proper health and safety information. Some may not have the expertise – others may not even know what it is they are supplying. *To check their information you must know the chemical composition of the product.*

For example, the label on one product advised users to follow a certain TLV (see page 51) but did not name the substance to which the TLV applied. When asked about this, the supplier admitted that he himself did not know what was in his product. His company had simply bought it from another supplier and resold it in smaller containers under a new label. Here is how their health and safety information had been produced:

'We asked the chemical company for *their* health and safety information which we took as it stood and retranscribed it. We sent it to the printer and told them to put it on the label . . . We didn't really think about it much . . . We got the [other company's] health and safety information and we stuck it on the label.'

The company's technical leaflet invited customers to contact it if more health and safety information was needed. What had happened to such requests?

'So far no-one has asked us. If they did we would probably have a heart attack and try and figure out what to send them.'

'You realise no-one knows what they are doing. It's very much a Heath-Robinson type of thing from our point of view and many others . . . 95 per cent of manufacturers in industry don't really consider it [the quality of information they supply] at all. They just hope someone doesn't come up with a complaint.'

While some data sheets are of a high standard, others play down the real hazard or contain serious mistakes. Data sheets may:

- Warn only about the short-term hazards of a substance (for example, fumes may cause irritation or sleepiness) but not of serious hazards (such as liver damage or cancer) of long-term exposure.

- Give no information at all about the dangers of highly toxic substances. Sometimes these may actually be described as 'safe' or 'harmless'.
- Give wrong figures for TLVs or provide information about chemicals that are not actually used in the product at all.
Examples of such data sheets are given later in this book. See *Examples 11, 15, 18* and *19*.

These errors were only noticed because the chemicals involved were named: their hazards could therefore be checked in other sources of information. If you cannot identify the composition of trade-named substances you will have no way of detecting such mistakes.

Trade secrets

The Health and Safety at Work Act does not require suppliers to disclose the composition of their products. In some cases, suppliers do provide this information – in other cases they argue that the composition of a product is a trade secret.

There is no exact definition of a trade secret in English law. Manufacturers may argue that any information about their products or business that they want to keep secret is in fact a 'trade secret'. But if a manufacturer wanted to claim legal protection for a chemical formulation which they considered to be a trade secret, they would have to convince the court that the information:

- gives them an advantage in trade over their competitors
- is unpatented (patented formulas are automatically published)
- is normally kept secret from competitors, and
- is not likely to be independently discovered by competitors, for example by reading the technical literature or by analysing the original product.

A skilled and determined chemical analyst can discover the composition of most chemical products. So, if a product is sold on the open market it is hard to keep its composition a secret. A state official from Oregon in the USA has commented:

'Our office has little or no sympathy with firms which claim that providing the common or chemical name (of hazardous ingredients in a product) will reveal their "secret" formulation . . . As a matter of fact many, if not most, secret formulations can be broken fairly easily using the sophisticated analytical techniques presently available to

Example 7. **Unnecessary secrets**

Social Audit examined the data sheets issued by 20 different adhesive manufacturers in 1979 to discover whether they identified the names of the solvents used. The manufacturers were also asked about their policies on disclosure.

- Nine out of the 20 refused to name the solvents or said they would only do so if pressed by a doctor or factory inspector.
- The remaining 11 companies regarded this information as public property. Most of them named the solvents on their data sheets – the rest said they would automatically disclose them to anyone who asked.

Although many companies refused to give customers this information, none of them claimed that real trade secrets were involved. All the manufacturers agreed that the solvent content could easily be discovered by simple analysis and one stated, 'Any chemist taking a specific adhesive would recognise the solvent just from the odour.'

Another manufacturer admitted: 'All our competitors have a pretty good idea of what we use and we have a pretty good idea of what they use.' Nevertheless, this company said it would refuse to tell a customer what solvent was used in one of its adhesive products.

those who really want to know.' Ralph M. Rodia, Assistant Manager, Occupational Health Section, State of Oregon, quoted in *Occupational Health,* March/April 1978, page 25.

There are plenty of analytical chemists who earn their living by analysing products for competitors who want to duplicate them. In the UK, consultant chemists state that they can identify all the ingredients in a mixture such as a paint or adhesive (except possibly for minute traces of new additives) for between £100 and £200, at 1980 prices. This cost would be trivial to any company thinking of duplicating one of its competitor's profitable products.

The fact that the manufacturer may withhold the name of the ingredients from a safety data sheet may deprive users of information they need for health and safety purposes. It is not likely to protect the product's identity from a determined competitor. See *Example 7.*

Some suppliers recognise that they can disclose substantial information about their products' composition without harming their own interests. One example is the International Paint Company whose disclosure policy is shown in *Example 8.*

Example 8. **International Paint Company's disclosure policy**

'Many customers seek further information on paint hazards. There are three levels of information:
1. general paint hazards
2. the specific problems of a particular product
3. the formulation of the product.

The small operator, such as a boat yard or vehicle refinisher will probably only be interested in (1). Medium-size customers including much of the engineering industry will want (2). Large companies will ask for (3) on the grounds that, as long as they know what materials they are dealing with, they are best able to decide on the degree of risk and appropriate precautions in their own plant. *This, by the way, is the policy adopted by IP towards its suppliers . . .*

If a customer asks for the formulation of a product for health and safety purposes then *we should provide as much information as a competent analyst could discover without great effort.* Effectively, this means we should provide:

Solvent content, that is, the chemical names and rough proportions of volatile components.

Resin type (e.g. 'oxidising alkyd', 'vinyl chloride/acetate copolymer', 'medium molecular-weight epoxy').

Pigment type (e.g. 'lead chromate', 'phthalocyanine blue', 'titanium dioxide').

Hardener type (e.g. 'Aromatic isocyanate adduct based on TDI', 'polyamide', 'sulphuric acid').

Any additive present in significant amounts which could have a bearing on the health and safety of the user.

This last item, of course, requires discretion to be carefully exercised . . .

A few large customers, particularly in the food packaging industry, will seek *more detailed information. If they require it for good reason, it should be freely given.'* (italics added)

4 Action on unidentified chemicals

The most realistic way to deal with this problem is to get your employer to adopt firm policies towards the suppliers of trade-named products.

Insist on full information

Get your employer to adopt a policy of not using trade-named substances unless their composition is fully known. Your aim should be to have this formally adopted as part of your employer's safety policy. Ask your employer to write to all suppliers of trade-named substances asking for the full composition. If necessary, your employer may need to tell them that unless they identify the ingredients you will stop using the product. Few suppliers will maintain a rigid secrecy policy if it loses them business.

Your employer should ask for all ingredients in a product, not merely those which the supplier considers hazardous. There is no single, generally accepted basis for distinguishing between 'hazardous' and 'non-hazardous' materials (see page 28). You can only decide whether a substance is likely to be hazardous when you know exactly where and how it is used. The *user* – that is you and your employer – not the *supplier*, should evaluate the possible hazard.

The supplier should be asked to give a rough indication of the proportions in which different ingredients are present in a product. Suppliers may consider the *exact* percentage composition to be sensitive information, and refuse to supply precise details. For health and safety purposes, an approximate figure (e.g. 'between 20 and 40 per cent' or 'less than 5 per cent') will usually be enough. See *Example 9*.

Suppliers may want to know exactly *why* you need this information. Your employer should explain the reasons and if necessary give an undertaking that the information will be used only for health and safety purposes and for no other reason.

If necessary, change product

If the supplier does not provide the necessary information ask your employer to look for an alternative product. But beware of changing to a product that is more dangerous than the original. Before deciding on an alternative product, make sure that you have adequate information about its composition, hazards and the measures needed to use it safely.

If there is no alternative product, it may be worth having the product analysed. If your employer has a chemical laboratory it may be able to identify the composition of chemical products. Alternatively, you may need to send a sample of the product to an outside analyst. If you suspect an immediate hazard to health

Example 9. **Data sheets: Identifying the product**

An extract from a basic health and safety data sheet is shown below.
The full data sheet is shown on pages 79–82.

If it is completed properly, you should find the following information about the identity of the product:
- **the product name (this could be the trade-name)**
- **a description of its appearance and odour**
  a list of ingredients, identifying each by its chemical name and
- **formula**
- **a rough idea of the proportions of each ingredient used**
- **details of any impurities; these may have their own toxic properties.**

HEALTH AND SAFETY INFORMATION

PRODUCT NAME	APPEARANCE
	ODOUR
SUPPLIER'S NAME & ADDRESS	EMERGENCY PHONE NO. (Day/Night/Weekend)
	ASK FOR

IMPORTANT: If any section of this form is not relevant or cannot be completed, the supplier should enter one of the following phrases: 'No Data', 'None/No Hazard', 'Not Applicable for following reason. . .'. If a box has been left blank, the user should check with the supplier to ensure that no oversight has occurred.

	CHEMICAL NAMES & SYNONYMS	FORMULAE	APPROXIMATE PROPORTIONS
INGREDIENTS			
IMPURITIES			

All ingredients should be listed. Generalisations such as 'hydrocarbons', 'alcohols', 'chlorinated solvents' are not sufficient. Proper chemical names and formulae are essential for evaluating toxicity.

from an unidentified chemical product, contact the Factory
Inspectorate. They may be prepared to analyse the product or to
provide you with other information. (See page 26 below.)

Investigate the product yourself

**If your employer is not prepared to act on unidentified chemicals
you may need to take steps yourself.** There are several things you
could do:

Contact the supplier. If your employer has not written to the supplier, it may be worth doing this yourself and asking for details of the product's composition. Not all suppliers will answer your questions – but some may. If you are not successful it may be worth asking your union's health and safety officer, or other official to do so for you.

Consult reference books. If the supplier of the product genuinely considers its composition to be a trade secret, the supplier won't have released it to anyone and it won't appear in any published source.

On the other hand, the composition may not be a real secret at all. The supplier may have withheld it from you simply because they hope to avoid what they see as unnecessary trouble. In this case, you may find details about the product's composition in a trade directory or chemical dictionary. Some possible sources are shown on pages 87–89.

In general, these sources are tedious to use and unrewarding. Although you may occasionally be lucky, your chances of getting the information in this way are not high.

Try and have the product analysed. The costs of having a product analysed will normally be too much for your branch funds, but your union's head office may be prepared to arrange this for you if there is a strong case. A university or polytechnic chemistry department will often have the equipment needed to analyse a product, and it may be well worth contacting staff or students to see if they are prepared to help you in this way.

Look for alternative products, and then try and persuade your employer to use them. You can identify possible alternatives by consulting trade directories or buyers' guides in a reference library. Each guide will deal with a particular industry or product – some are listed on pages 88–89.

Once you have identified a possible alternative, write to the supplier and ask if the product is suitable and if you can have full health and safety information. Suppliers may not be used to dealing with trade-union representatives, but if they think that your letter may bring them a new customer they will probably take it very seriously. A letter you can use when writing to suppliers is shown in *Example 10.*

Ban the product

If nothing else works you may want to discuss with your members the possibility of refusing to handle unidentified chemical products.

Example 10. **Letter asking suppliers about possible alternatives to an unidentified trade-name product**

The Sales Manager
Company name and address   *date*

Dear Sir or Madam,

I am a trade union safety representative at *(name of your place of work)*, and am writing to ask whether you have a product suitable for use as *(describe exact purpose of product)* and to ask for health and safety details about any such product.

The product we are presently using is not, in our opinion, accompanied by adequate health and safety information. In particular, its ingredients are not identified and we have therefore been unable to confirm that the health and safety information supplied is satisfactory.

It is the policy of our trade union branch that members should not work with substances of unknown composition. We therefore would like to replace the product we now use by one whose ingredients are identified and is accompanied by adequate health and safety information.

We would like to receive such information about your product in order to consider recommending its use to our management.

I would be very grateful if you would send me your technical data and full health and safety information concerning your product. The latter should include:

1. The chemical names of all ingredients present and an approximate indication of the proportions in which they are present.

2. Details of the potential harmful effects caused by over-exposure to each ingredient, including long-term as well as short-term hazards, by all routes of exposure.

3. The precautions needed to ensure that the product can be used without risks to health.

Any information you supply will be used for health and safety purposes only and will not be used or divulged for any other purpose.

I shall appreciate your help with this enquiry and look forward to hearing from you.

Yours sincerely,

Your name

5 The factory inspector

If lack of information prevents you from doing your job, or could lead to an immediate hazard to health, contact the factory inspector. This applies whether or not trade-name products are involved.

A factory inspector must disclose information when:

'it is necessary to do so for the purpose of assisting in keeping persons (or the representatives of persons) employed at any premises adequately informed about matters affecting their health, safety and welfare.' Health and Safety at Work Act, section 28(8).

According to the same section of the Act, there are two kinds of information that an inspector must disclose in these circumstances:

'1. factual information obtained by him . . . which relates to those premises or anything which was or is therein or was or is being done therein; and

2. information with respect to any action which he has taken or proposes to take in or in connection with those premises in the performance of his functions'.

In general, it is not normally worth approaching a factory inspector for information unless you have already tried – and failed – to get it from your employer.

'The role of inspectors is to ensure that employers carry out their duty of providing information. Inspectors are not, in general, required to duplicate or provide a substitute for information which has been (or should have been) disclosed by the employer in persuance of the (employer's) primary duty under section 2(2)(c). *An exception would be where there exists an immediate and significant threat to health and safety which, in the inspector's judgement, requires immediate disclosure to the workforce'.* (italics added). Letter from HSE press office to Social Audit, 9 December 1980.

Trade secrets and the inspector

Factory inspectors will normally be very reluctant to disclose any information which a supplier claims is a trade secret. But section 28(8) of the Act requires them to provide factual information about hazards when it is 'necessary to do so' in order to help keep employees adequately informed.

So if an inspector decides – or is persuaded – that you need to know the names of chemicals in a trade-named product, he or she must give them to you – trade secret or not.

Inspectors are most likely to give you this information if they are taking enforcement action in connection with the product, taking samples away to be analysed, or instructing your employer to monitor concentrations in the air.

Where the chemicals involved are covered by special regulations or codes of practice (e.g. asbestos or lead) inspectors may decide that workers must be told what they are working with. They may sometimes do this with other substances of well-known hazard where they feel that users are more likely to follow safety precautions if they know the name of the substance involved.

But these are not the only times when safety representatives need to know the names of chemicals in the workplace. **This book suggests that it is extremely difficult to control chemical hazards without knowing the names of the chemicals involved. You should argue that as a general rule you need to know the composition of the products used in your workplace.**

Factory inspectors may not always agree. They may suggest that as long as you know the *hazards* of the substance you don't need to have its *name*. You may have to persuade them of your case if you are to get the information.

If you are approaching a factory inspector for information, be ready to demonstrate two things:
1. That you need the information to do your job properly. The information should be 'necessary' to you – not just 'possibly helpful' or 'interesting'. Be ready to explain why you need it and how you are going to use it.
2. That you have been unable to get this information from your employer, or from any other source (such as the supplier) which you may have tried.

Confidential information

Any information that the factory inspector or your employer gives you in connection with your functions as a safety representative must *only* be used for health and safety purposes. A safety representative who discloses such information for any other purpose may have committed an offence under section 28(2) of the Act.

The restriction will not prevent you from doing anything you need to do as a safety representative – it may even work to your advantage. Your employer or a supplier may argue that they can't risk giving you information for fear that you might leak it to a competitor. You can point out that you are bound by law not to misuse the information in this way.

6 Hazard assessments

One of the problems you may find in the information you get from a supplier is that there is no specific information about the hazard at all. Instead, the data sheet may use general statements such as 'toxic', 'safe if properly used with good ventilation', or 'harmful by inhalation'.

There are two things wrong with such assessments:
- They are inadequate. You should be getting a specific description of the kind of injury that could occur.
- They can be misleading. The section below explains why.

'Safe' substances

No substance is in itself 'safe', 'harmless', or 'non toxic'. Almost any substance can be dangerous in excess. Equally, even the most toxic substance can usually be used safely – although this may sometimes involve extremely rigorous measures.

For most chemicals, it is not the substance itself which is 'safe' or 'dangerous' but the dose or concentration to which you are exposed. Cancer-causing substances are one exception to this rule. As far as we know, there are no 'safe levels' for these substances – they are always dangerous.

But most substances can usually be used quite safely as long as exposure levels are low. However, as the concentration increases, so does the risk. For example, a certain amount of a given solvent may be safe to use in a large and well-ventilated workroom but be lethal if in a small, unventilated space such as the inside of a boiler.

Reference books on chemical hazards therefore give a very strong warning on this point:

'the unqualified use of terms such as "toxic", "non toxic" and "safe" as applied to industrial air contaminants can create

Example 11. 'Safe' substances

1. **Supplier's data sheet: starch powder spray**

   'The spray materials are *intrinsically harmless* – nevertheless it is wise to avoid excessive inhalation.'

   Encyclopaedia of Occupational Safety and Health. Entry on 'starch'.

   'it may aggravate certain lung conditions such as emphysema. Individuals sensitive to dust should not work in dusty areas . . . Some workers may also contract dermatitis through handling starch products.'

2. **Supplier's data sheet: Barytes**

   '*non-toxic* insoluble salt'

   Later in same data sheet

   'dust inhalation can result in long term *pneumoconiosis*'

3. **Supplier's advertisement:**

   'Safe, Fast, Economic. The *Safe* Chemical Cleaner . . . Very much safer than the old "neat acid" cleansers'.

   Same supplier's data sheet for the product

   'strongly acidic and will attack and damage skin. Ingestion . . . will cause severe burning of mouth throat and digestive tract. Prolonged inhalation . . . will cause irritation and discomfort and could result in serious damage to the lungs.'

false and dangerous illusions'. International Labour Office, *Encyclopaedia of Occupational Safety and Health.*
Unfortunately, as *Example 11* illustrates, some suppliers make precisely these claims for their products.

'Safe if properly used'

Some data sheets stop short of calling the product 'safe' but instead say that is is 'safe if properly used'. This is of course true of nearly everything, and in itself tells you nothing.

The basic expression can be spruced up a little without in any way adding to its meaning. For example the data sheet may

● *Example 12.* **'Safe if properly used'**

A supplier has a policy of deciding themselves whether their product's ingredients are 'harmful' or 'harmless'. If they decide the ingredients are 'harmless', they are not identified on the health and safety data sheet, which is left almost completely blank. The only information it gives is fire hazard data, and the following statement:

> *'Health hazard.* This product is formulated on materials that are not thought to be harmful, or are not present in sufficient quantities to be harmful, if used properly under conditions of good industrial hygiene.'

According to the supplier, this statement would normally be used for substances like white spirit. **However, not every one would agree that white spirit is harmless.** Although it is not thought of as highly toxic it is, like other solvents, irritating and narcotic at high concentrations. The Paint Research Association has reported that after painting a 'normally ventilated living room' with a white spirit based paint, the air in the room could contain solvent concentrations that are eleven times greater than the Threshold Limit Value (TLV). They concluded that 'white spirit as a paint solvent can present a toxic hazard if ventilation is inadequate'.

White spirit has other hazards. In October 1979, Esso Chemicals informed its customers that 'slight kidney damage' had been found in animals exposed to a white spirit type solvent. It was significant that damage had occurred at low concentrations – 100 ppm, the then TLV.

Users of this supplier's products would not be told when white spirit was present. According to the supplier: 'We are not required to disclose what the materials are under any circumstances. If it's a "no hazard" sheet, then it's a "no hazard" sheet.'

Some users may well feel that under certain conditions white spirit could create a hazard: but they would have no way of checking the supplier's claim that the product contained only harmless ingredients.

acknowledge that there could be some (unspecified) hazard if the (undefined) precautions are not followed. One supplier's data sheets advise users that:

> 'Provided *reasonable* care is taken the product does not present a *serious* risk . . . inhalation risks are *minor* in *good* ventilated conditions.' (italics added)

A statement like this is useless unless the key words are properly defined. The risks of *any* substance will be 'minor' if the ventilation system is 'good' enough. This would apply equally to water mist or cyanide vapour!

The example above was taken from a data sheet on an unidentified trade-named product. This makes it particularly dangerous – because users have no way of checking for themselves on the chemical's real hazards. See *Example 12*.

Toxic hazard ratings

A common way of assessing chemical hazards is to use toxicity ratings. Substances may be classified as having 'slight', 'moderate' or 'high' toxicity. The labelling regulations require ratings such as 'toxic', 'harmful' or 'irritant' to be put on container labels. In some systems, the codes are numbers (e.g. 1 = low hazard, 4 = high hazard) or colours (green = little hazard, red = danger).

Hazard ratings can be very useful – but there are several possible drawbacks.

One of the dangers is that people may be misled because they do not understand the basis of the ratings. For example, many systems are based on chemicals' 'LD50' values. The LD50 is the lethal dose that will kill 50% of a group of exposed animals.

Unfortunately, the LD50 of a substance gives no clue to its other toxic properties. If a substance is classified as a 'low' hazard on the basis of its LD50 all this means is that you won't be instantly killed if you swallow a little of it. The substance could still be highly irritating to inhale, a powerful narcotic or cause disabling disease or cancer.

Another danger is that the person who classifies the chemicals may be doing so arbitrarily. They may have no objective basis for allocating ratings, and may be using them in their own idiosyncratic way. What you consider to be a serious hazard, they may classify as 'minor'. See *Example 13*.

Hazard ratings can be valuable in warning users when they are dealing with particularly dangerous substances. But you should be very careful about relying on any rating unless you:

- understand the basis of the classification system – and its limitations
- know the meaning of each rating
- have access to full information on the hazards of the substance.

7 A full account of the hazards

For each substance you use at work, you should be given a specific and factual account of the toxic hazards.
You should be told:

1. The first symptoms of overexposure to the substance and the consequences of severe overexposure.
2. What dose, concentration or conditions of exposure are likely to cause injury.
3. The consequences of both short-term and long-term exposure.
4. The effects of the chemical by each of its possible routes of entry to the body.
5. The hazards of all ingredients in, or likely to be formed from, the product.

Note how the data sheet shown in *Example 14* covers each of these points.

● *Example 14.* **Data sheets: a full account of the hazards**

An extract from a basic data sheet is shown below. The full data sheet is shown on pages 79–82.

Note how the data sheet covers the five basic points listed on page 32.

4.
HEALTH
HAZARD

	EFFECTS OF SHORT-TERM EXPOSURE for each ingredient	EFFECTS OF LONG-TERM EXPOSURE for each ingredient	1ST DETECTABLE SIGNS OF OVEREXPOSURE Important: the absence of these signs does not necessarily mean conditions are safe!
	Wherever possible, the minimum concentration/exposure period thought to be capable of producing ill-effects should be specified.		
IF INHALED			
IF SWALLOWED			
IF ABSORBED THROUGH SKIN			
ON SKIN			
IN EYE			
	'NO HAZARD KNOWN' indicates that the substance has been tested and no hazard found. 'NO INFORMATION' indicates that the substance has not been tested. It should be treated as hazardous.		

Symptoms of overexposure

You should be told both the first symptoms of overexposure and the consequences of severe overexposure.

This will allow you to judge for yourself how dangerous the substance is – and to spot any signs of overexposure at the first possible opportunity. The importance of this information can be illustrated by looking at the narcotic effects of solvents.

A narcotic is a substance which can produce unconsciousness. Its effects can be divided into two phases:

1. In the early phase, the exposed person may feel dizzy, drowsy, light-headed or weak. There may be unpleasant effects such as headache or nausea.
2. If exposure continues, or if it is very much higher even for a short time, the danger is much greater. The exposed person may collapse, and if not rescued, paralysis, coma and even death may follow.

A solvent data sheet that warned only about the possibility of unconsciousness or death would be accurate – but incomplete. Users must be warned about the early symptoms so that they can recognise them if they occur and take immediate steps to end or reduce the exposure. Without this warning, some people may not connect the symptoms with the cause.

Few chemicals cause startlingly unusual ill-effects – the symptoms are usually very similar to those of 'normal' illness. If you haven't been told how to recognise overexposure you may mistake the symptoms for signs that you are coming down with a cold, or suffering from stomach upset or a hangover. As a result you may carry on working in conditions that are unhealthy or possibly even a threat to your life.

On the other hand, if the data sheet warned only about headache, dizziness or drowsiness it might suggest that these effects were the worst that could happen. You might tolerate the discomfort without realising that these are danger signs, and that further exposure could have very serious effects.

The account of the hazards given by 45 suppliers of solvents or solvented products was examined by Social Audit in 1979. **Less than a quarter of them gave an adequate description of the solvent hazards.** A selection of the findings are shown in *Example 15*.

Some of these data sheets gave no information on the hazards at all. Even data sheets for extremely toxic substances sometimes gave no information about the hazard. See *Example 16*.

Harmful concentrations

You should be told the dose, concentration or conditions of exposure that are likely to cause injury.

It is important to have some idea of the conditions likely to cause injury:
- At low levels of exposure, a substance may have no harmful effects – yet at high levels it may cause devastating injury.

For some substances, just the briefest whiff of fumes may cause injury. For others, no harm occurs unless a person has been working for years in heavily contaminated conditions.

Wherever possible you should be told the concentration and period of exposure likely to be harmful. This is particularly important for inhalation hazards.

Your employer should be monitoring contamination levels in the air and giving you copies of the results. By comparing the measured levels with those known to be harmful, you can tell how likely you are to be at risk.

Instead of giving actual figures, data sheets – and reference books – sometimes use terms like 'moderate exposure', or 'high concentrations'. This can be confusing. For example, the two accounts below are taken from suppliers' data sheets for toluene. Both claim to describe the consequences of inhaling 'high' concentrations:

'Prolonged exposure to *high* solvent vapour concentrations can cause headache, dizziness, nausea and fatigue.'

'*High* concentrations can cause depression of the central nervous system terminating in narcosis and respiratory paralysis.'

Example 16. **Even for highly toxic chemicals, suppliers may give no description of the hazard**

The hazards of cadmium compounds, as described by (1) a standard reference book and (2) a supplier, are shown below. The complete 'Health Hazard' section of the supplier's data sheet has been reproduced.

1. **Standard reference book**
   'Cadmium compounds. The inhalation of fumes or dusts of cadmium primarily affect the respiratory tract; the kidneys may also be affected. Even brief exposure to high concentration may result in pulmonary edema and death . . . Inhalation of dust or fumes may cause dryness of the throat, cough, headache, a sense of constriction in the chest, shortness of breath (dyspnea) and vomiting. More severe exposure results in marked lung changes, with persistent cough, pain in the chest, severe dyspnea and prostration which may terminate fatally . . . These symptoms are usually delayed for some hours after exposure, and *fatal concentrations may be breathed without sufficient discomfort to warn the workman to leave the exposure* . . . Many cadmium compounds are experimental carcinogens . . .' N. I. Sax, *Dangerous Properties of Industrial Materials,* 5th edition 1979.

2. **Suppliers' data sheet for cadmium chloride**

SECTION V. HEALTH HAZARD
THRESHOLD LIMIT VALUE 0.2 mg/M^3 orl-rat LD_{50}: 88 mg/kg
HEALTH HAZARDS:
FIRST AID PROCEDURES: If inhaled remove to fresh air. If not breathing, give artificial respiration. If breathing is difficult, give oxygen. If swallowed, if conscious, immediately induce vomiting. Call a physician.

Clearly, the second account is describing much 'higher' concentrations than the first. Only if the actual figures are given – as they are in *Example 17* – will you be able to judge whether levels found in your own workplace are likely to be dangerous.

It is not always possible to say which concentrations of a substance are dangerous and which are not. We rarely have

Example 17. **Toluene exposure: dose and effect**

Concentration (parts per million)	Period of exposure	Effects
50–200 ppm	6–8 hours daily for 1–3 weeks	headache, tiredness, loss of appetite (although these effects may have been caused by factors other than the toluene exposure).
200–500 ppm	ditto	the above symptoms *plus* poor coordination, reduced reaction time, momentary loss of memory.
500–1,500 ppm	ditto	extreme weakness
10,000–30,000 ppm	not known	collapse and unconsciousness

Source: US National Institute for Occupational Safety and Health, *Occupational Exposure to Toluene: Criteria for a Recommended Standard,* 1973, pages 21–23.

complete information about the hazards of particular chemicals. Even those chemicals that have been in use for many years are continually being found to have new hazards, or to be dangerous at concentrations previously thought to be safe.

The Health and Safety Executive therefore advises users: 'to adopt a general precautionary policy for controlling the use of *all* substances, whether or not they are known to have any harmful effects . . . Where there are no known toxic effects, there should still be a policy of keeping exposure as low as is reasonably practicable.' 'Toxic Substances: A Precautionary Policy', Health and Safety Executive, Guidance Note EH 18.

Long-term effects

You should be told the effects of both short-term and long-term exposure to the substance.

A single substance may have different effects, depending on the length of time you are exposed to it.

Brief exposure to many substances produces an immediate effect. For example, irritation and choking caused by breathing ammonia fumes; dizziness or unconsciousness from inhaling solvent vapours; or a burn caused by a splash of acid on the skin.

Repeated exposure over a long period may lead to different kinds of injury. These often develop gradually without any detectable signs in the early stages. Sometimes the illness takes many years to appear, and may be caused by exposures that are too small to have any immediate warning effects at the time. Examples of these long term effects include lung diseases such as asbestosis or pneumoconiosis, many skin disorders, and cancer.

The same substance may have both short-term and long-term effects. Benzene causes narcosis in short exposures; long-term exposure may cause blood diseases such as leukemia. Swallowing a single high dose of the herbicide diquat may be lethal; repeated smaller doses over a long period cause cataracts of the eye. Occasional splashes of mineral oil on the skin may have no significant effect; repeated exposure may cause skin disorders and possibly skin cancer.

Data sheets should tell you about *both* kinds of effects.

In practice, many data sheets only describe the short-term effects of substances. This can be misleading because **some chemicals cause long-term disease at concentrations which are too low to have any immediate warning effect.** See *Example 18*.

For other substances, the long-term effects occur only at concentrations above those needed to produce an immediate effect. If precautions are good enough to prevent the short-term effects, there should be no long-term hazard. Even so, a warning about the long-term effects is essential: otherwise workers may tolerate mild short-term effects without realising that there is also a hidden hazard. See *Example 19*.

Routes of exposure

You should be told about the potential hazard by each possible route of exposure.

Substances may enter the body by three different routes. They may be:

- inhaled
- swallowed
- absorbed through the skin.

They may also attack the surface of the body – the skin and the eyes.

Sometimes these hazards are obvious. A dust or gas can obviously be inhaled, a liquid can be splashed onto the body, and a chemical may be swallowed if it is transferred from unwashed hands onto food, drink or cigarettes. Some of the other hazards are less obvious.

Skin absorption
Many chemicals can be absorbed into the body through the unbroken skin. For a highly toxic substance like phenol (1 gram is enough to kill) a person who has been heavily splashed may absorb a lethal dose through the skin in a matter of minutes.

In some cases, even the *vapour* of a substance may be absorbed through the skin. People exposed to aniline, nitroben-

● *Example 19.* **Long-term hazards of perchloroethylene**

Short-term exposure to the solvent perchloroethylene causes narcosis. Severe or prolonged exposure causes liver damage. This example does not discuss the evidence that perchloroethylene causes cancer in animal experiments.

Perchloroethylene only seems to damage the liver if concentrations are high enough to cause narcotic symptoms. If proper steps to prevent the short-term hazard are taken, there should be no risk of liver damage.

Suppliers must still warn of the long-term risk: they cannot assume that a warning of the narcotic hazard alone will be enough. The case history below shows that without such warning workers may learn – or be persuaded – to live with a narcotic hazard.

A 1953 report on the health of workers using perchloroethylene as a degreaser found: 'Complaints of headache, nausea, lightheadedness, dizziness, tiredness, hangover and feelings of intoxication were listed repeatedly in the occupational histories. A few workers passed out after exposure but recovered quickly afterwards. One worker reported that his eyes "did not coordinate"; another said that he "could not hit the spot". Two men had laughing spells; another learned to anticipate fainting spells and avoid them by going out into the fresh air.'

These workers had clearly adapted to excessive exposures, learning to anticipate and avoid the worst effects. This continued until one man was eventually taken to hospital vomiting blood, where he was found to have a damaged liver. His colleagues were then examined and 2 out of the 6 men who had used perchloroethylene for more than a year also showed signs of liver damage. H. R. Coler and H. R. Rossmiller, *Archives of Industrial Hygiene and Occupational Medicine,* 1953, vol. 8, pages 227–33.

In 1978 – 25 years after this report – one of the two major suppliers of perchloroethylene in the UK still warned users only of the short-term hazard:

'Inhalation of high concentrations . . . of perchloroethylene vapour will cause drowsiness, headaches and giddiness and may lead to unconsciousness or prove suddenly fatal if the exposure has been severe.' *(ICI Ltd)*

'can produce varying degrees of anaesthesia . . . lightheadedness, impaired coordination, dizziness, etc. . . . . exposure to concentrations causing dizziness might produce *some degree of liver injury in susceptible individuals.' (Dow Chemical Company Ltd)*

zene or phenol vapours may absorb as much through their skin as through their lungs – and normal work clothing gives very little form of protection.

To tell which of the commoner substances are absorbed through the skin, look at the list of Threshold Limit Values published each year by the Health and Safety Executive (Guidance Note EH/15). Those which can easily be absorbed through the skin have the word 'Skin' entered after their names.

Inhalation hazards from liquids

All liquids – or any solids being melted – give off vapours which can be inhaled. Some (like petrol or many solvents) evaporate quickly at room temperature so they may normally present an inhalation hazard. Even slowly evaporating liquids (like mercury or oils) give off some vapours at room temperature. All liquids evaporate more quickly if they are heated, so the possibility of risk always increases at higher temperatures. More information about the volatility of liquids is given on page 56.

If a liquid is sprayed, or comes into contact with fast moving machinery parts, then a *mist* of fine droplets is formed in the air. Mists can be inhaled – and may be harmful. The data sheet on a cutting oil which gives no information about an inhalation hazard on the grounds that the oil is 'relatively unvolatile' is therefore dangerously missing the point.

Data sheets should cover all potential routes of exposure when describing:
- the hazards of the substance
- protective measures needed
- first-aid treatment.

Note how this is done in sections 3, 4 and 10 of the data sheet shown on pages 79–82. The importance of this is illustrated in *Example 20*.

Mixtures, impurities and additives

You should be told the hazards of all ingredients in the product or likely to be formed from it.

Mixtures

Many industrial products are not single pure substances but mixtures of several. Each of the ingredients may have its own separate toxic properties.

Example 20. **Routes of exposure**

The extracts below are taken from two data sheets on the same chemical – an isocyanate called MDI. (Full name: diphenyl methane diisocyanate). In each case, the data sheet's full first-aid section is shown.

The first data sheet's advice deals only with splashes on the skin. It gives no advice to anyone who may have to deal with an emergency involving any of the other three possible routes of exposure.

Data sheet 1

'The isocyanate activator is a powerful chemical which should not be allowed in contact with the skin, and particularly the eyes. Goggles and gloves should be worn when handling, and any spillage on the skin should be wiped off immediately and the area washed with soap and water.'

Data sheet 2

'*Eye contact.* Flush out the eyes immediately with copious amounts of water for 15 minutes. Obtain medical attention.

Skin contact. Remove all contaminated clothing immediately and rub the affected area with a 30/70 isopropyl alcohol/water mixture. Wash with soap and water. Obtain medical attention if large areas of the skin have been affected.

Inhalation. Remove affected person to fresh air immediately and obtain medical attention.

Ingestion. The oral toxicity is low but if substantial amounts have been swallowed, induce vomiting by giving one or more glasses of water each containing 2 tablespoonfuls of common salt and/or by depressing the back of the tongue with a finger. Obtain medical attention. **Do not** give anything by mouth to an unconscious person.'

Some data sheets deal with the hazards of only one of the ingredients in a mixture – and leave the others out. The ingredient described may not be the most toxic one – it may be the one present in the largest amounts, or the one that is most important in terms of the product's functions. See *Example 21.*

Impurities

Substances frequently contain impurities – and often the impurity is more toxic than the main ingredient. For example, the weedkiller 2,4,5-T is normally contaminated by traces of dioxin – a highly toxic chemical which causes birth defects. Some grades of zinc oxide (which itself is not very harmful) are contaminated with traces of very toxic metals such as cadmium

---

Example 21. **Mixtures**

Extracts from a number of data sheets are shown below. In each case, the product involved contains a mixture of an isocyanate and a solvent. The inhalation hazards of the two are quite distinct.

Isocyanates irritate the throat and lungs. Exposure may cause asthma attacks. Some people may become 'sensitised' – allergic – to isocyanates and be unable to tolerate even the most minute traces in the air.

Solvents are narcotic. Their vapours cause dizziness, drowsiness and unconsciousness. Some also have long-term hazards.

In each of the extracts below, judge for yourself how adequately the data sheet describes the hazards of the two ingredients.

1. 'Effects of overexposure: intoxication effect.'
2. 'The solvents used are potentially irritating.'
3. 'Effects of overexposure: TDI (an isocyanate) is toxic by inhalation. Emergency and First Aid: If subject becomes unconscious apply artificial respiration.'
4. 'Due to the low (isocyanate) content there is only a slight danger of irritation being caused by inhalation or sensitizing.'
5. 'Two potential hazards exist with these products. First from the organic solvents present in some, and secondly from small amounts of isocyanates present . . .'

---

or lead. Toluene – whose main hazard is as a narcotic – was for many years believed to cause blood disorders which were in fact caused by benzene impurities.

Additives

Many products contain small amounts of different additives, used to alter or improve their properties. For example, lubricating oils may contain chemicals designed to improve their flow, prevent foaming, stop bacterial growth or prevent the oil from breaking down under high temperature or pressure. The additives may have their own toxic properties – though they may be used only in minute quantities.

Decomposition and reaction products

Many chemicals can suddenly change their composition, creating a new hazard. The new products formed may be more toxic than the original – or the change may occur with the violent release of energy, leading to an explosion or fire.

Example 22. **Decomposition and reaction products**

The solvent trichloroethylene (TCE) readily decomposes. Oxygen, light, moisture, impurities and high temperature all cause TCE to break down, forming toxic and corrosive products such as hydrochloric acid and phosgene – a chemical warfare agent used in the first world war. To prevent this decomposition, stabilisers – which may be toxic in themselves – are added to commercial TCE, but even these are ineffective at high temperatures.

TCE has been used as an anaesthetic in surgical operations. The TCE was recirculated during the operation, and was first purified by passing through a soda-lime cannister to remove the patient's exhaled carbon dioxide.

It was later learnt that trichloroethylene and soda-lime react together – forming an extremely toxic compound called dichloroacetylene. Dichloroacetylene poisoning was blamed for two deaths and several cases of illness in people recovering from operations in a London hospital during 1943.

The US National Institute for Occupational Safety and Health warns: 'It should thus be obvious that the hazard from TCE must be judged not only on the basis of its own toxicity but also on those of the products that may be produced by reaction with other chemicals present during the processes in which TCE is used.' *Source:* US National Institute for Occupational Safety and Health, *Trichloroethylene: Special Occupational Hazard Review with Recommendations,* 1978.

Usually, such changes will only occur in the presence of other substances. Many substances will react if they come in contact with specific chemicals or even in some cases with air or water. See *Example 22.* A particularly dangerous class of materials are the 'oxidising agents'. These can react with combustible materials or substances producing an explosive fire.

Some 'unstable' substances can change their composition without contact with another substance. A change in the temperature or pressure may be enough to cause these substances to explode, decompose or 'polymerise' – react with themselves to form long chains built up from the original. *Example 23* shows what information suppliers' data sheets should give about decomposition and reaction products.

Example 23. **Data sheets: decomposition and reaction hazards**

An extract from a basic sheet is shown below. The full data sheet is shown on pages 79–82.

If the data sheet is properly completed, it should tell you:
- whether, and under what conditions, the substance is likely to decompose, polymerise or react with other substances
- what hazards might result
- what special storage and handling measures should be adopted.

11.
STORAGE

STORAGE & HANDLING MEASURES	
SPECIAL CONTAINER DESIGN & MATERIALS	
DECOMPOSITION PRODUCTS & HAZARDS	CONDITIONS LEADING TO DECOMPOSITION
POLYMERISATION PRODUCTS & HAZARDS	CONDITIONS LEADING TO POLYMERISATION
INCOMPATIBLE SUBSTANCES & HAZARDS	

8 Untested chemicals

You may not always be able to get full information on a chemical's hazards – because many chemicals have never been fully tested.

This should improve a little, because chemical manufacturers are now required by law to carry out research into the toxicity of their products. The basic duty comes from section 6(5) of the Health and Safety at Work Act – shown on page 91.

The notification of new substances regulations

The testing requirement will have the most impact on *new* chemicals. Regulations in draft at the time of writing will require manufacturers to provide certain toxicity data to the Health and

Safety Executive (HSE) before they are allowed to market a new chemical.

The new notification scheme is not designed to 'approve' or ban new substances – its aim is only to generate information. When the scheme is in operation, you may be told that a chemical you are using has been 'notified' to the HSE. This will only mean that certain basic research has been carried out. It will not mean that the chemical's hazards have been fully investigated or that the substance has been 'cleared for use' by the HSE.

Four basic sets of tests will have to be carried out on new chemicals:

1. **Acute toxicity tests.** These investigate the effects of a single dose of the substance on animals when swallowed, inhaled or absorbed through the skin. The tests will usually determine the lethal dose (LD50) and give a very rough idea of major non-lethal effects.

2. **Skin and eye tests.** These will determine whether the substance irritates the skin or eyes and whether it causes an allergic skin response ('skin sensitisation').

3. **Sub-acute toxicity tests.** In these tests, animals are exposed to regular doses of the substance for at least 4 weeks. This may give some idea of the effects of repeated exposure in humans. But of course, humans may not react in the same way as animals – and some harmful effects will be missed because they may only develop after months or years of exposure.

4. **Mutagenicity tests.** These are short tests used to detect possible carcinogens – cancer causing substances. Bacteria or cell cultures are exposed to the substance to see whether mutations – changes in the genetic material – occur. Most of the substances that cause mutations in these tests are capable of causing cancer in animals, and possibly in humans.

These are the basic tests that will have to be used on all new substances when the regulations come into force. They will give an indication – but not a full account – of the hazards.

If the substance is marketed in very large quantities, or if the HSE suspects it may be particularly toxic, further tests may be required.

These may include reproductive studies to see whether the chemical interferes with fertility or causes birth defects (such substances are called 'teratogens'). Studies may investigate the long-term ('chronic') effects of the chemical or the possibility that they cause cancer.

Example 24. **Untested chemicals**

Dr Alf Spinks, former director of research at ICI, told the annual meeting of the Royal Institute of Chemistry and the Chemical Society that it would take about 30 years and cost about £5 billion to test all the untested chemicals in daily use to see whether they could cause cancer. Only 6,000 of the 30,000 chemicals in daily use have so far been examined for their ability to cause cancer, and about 1,000 of the 6,000 tested have been found to be positive. *'Thus you could argue that 4,000 carcinogens remain to be detected among industrial chemicals,'* he said when giving the presidential address to the Institute. *Guardian,* 10 April 1980.

The lack of testing

Many substances now in use have never been tested for long-term effects. A former chairman of the US body which sets the TLV figures has commented:

'chronic animal inhalation toxicity ... data are in short supply because industries either do not develop long-term studies, or if they do, more often than not do not see fit to release the data in the open literature.' H. E. Stokinger, *Archives of Environmental Health,* vol. 19, August 1969, pages 277–81.

Because animal tests may not have been done in the past, we have had no advance warning of the possible hazards of many chemicals. See *Example 24.* Much of the information we do have has come from cases of human exposure. Sometimes the hazards have been discovered only after cases of poisoning amongst industrial workers have been detected – in other cases they are spotted purely by chance. See *Example 25.*

Systematic studies of the health of large groups of exposed workers ('epidemiological' studies) are a much more effective way of detecting these hazards – but few such studies are carried out. In 1977, Dr Guy Parkes, director of the British Rubber Manufacturers' Association's health research unit warned that:

'It is impossible to escape the conclusion that the principal cause of our past failures to identify the existence of an occupational cancer hazard lies quite simply in the fact that we have not looked for it ... epidemiological studies recently carried out in my own industry have indicated the existence of just such unsuspected cancer excesses, and this finding

Example 25. **New health hazards may be discovered completely by chance**

Methylene chloride has traditionally been thought of as one of the least toxic of the chlorinated solvents, although it can cause narcosis and, if exposure is severe enough, liver damage. However, in the early 1970s a new and completely unsuspected hazard was discovered.

A team of researchers were studying the effect of carbon monoxide on the blood and measuring the levels of the compound formed as a result, carboxyhaemoglobin (COHb). Most of the team gave samples of their own blood for analysis every Monday morning. The study proceeded normally until one Monday morning when the COHb level of one of the researchers, Dr Terrance Fisher, was found to be seven times its normal level. Despite extensive investigation, no source of carbon monoxide could be found in his home. The next Monday, his blood COHb level was normal, but a week later it was again very high.

After a good deal of thought, Dr Fisher realised that the only activity the two weekends had in common was his use of a paint stripper containing methylene chloride. Although the members of his team assured him that methylene chloride could have no effect on the COHb level, Dr Fisher insisted on exposing himself to a known level of the solvent in the laboratory. His COHb level immediately went up.

Further research confirmed that methylene chloride led to the formation of COHb in the blood and interfered with its ability to carry oxygen. Methylene chloride can produce an effect similar to carbon monoxide poisoning – and a number of deaths from heart attacks have since been reported in people using methylene chloride paint strippers. As a result of these findings the TLV (see page 51) for methylene chloride was reduced to one-fifth of its previous level.

Source: Jack E. Peterson, *Industrial Health,* Prentice-Hall, 1977.

must arouse the suspicion that if similar work were to be carried out elsewhere similar findings would probably result.'

Data sheets and untested chemicals

If a data sheet makes no reference to the possibility of a long-term hazard, it is safest to assume either that:

- the substance is untested – and therefore potentially dangerous, or
- a hazard is known, but not described. See *Examples 16, 18* and *19.*

Of course, the lack of information could mean that the substance has been tested and no hazard found. But if such results have been found, suppliers normally say so emphatically.

Ideally, a data sheet should tell you (1) what long-term hazards, if any, are known, and (2) how thoroughly the possibility of such hazards has been investigated. Note how this is done in *Example 26.*

The data sheet on pages 79–82 is designed to encourage suppliers to provide this information. If a supplier has no information about any long-term hazard, they should complete Section 4 of the data sheet with one of two phrases:

If the substance has been tested, they should enter
'no hazard known'
If the substance has not been tested, they should enter
'no information available'

Then in Section 5 of the data sheet, the supplier should show which tests have been carried out. See *Example 27.*

● *Example 27.* **Data sheets: toxicity testing**

An extract from a basic health and safety data sheet is shown below. The full data sheet is given on pages 79–82.

If the data sheet is properly completed, it should tell you what tests have – and have not – been carried out on the product.

5.
EXTENT OF
TESTING

The table below shows which toxicity tests have been carried out on the product and/or its individual ingredients. The tests listed are those that will be required for new chemicals under the proposed Notification of New Substances Regulations. Tests 1-6 will be required for all new substances. For some substances, Tests 7-10 may also be required.

Where a particular test has been carried out on the product or an individual ingredient, a cross should be entered in the appropriate box. A cross merely indicates that a test has been carried out: it does not describe the results of the test.

ANIMAL DATA			Pro-duct	Ingredient								Pro-duct	Ingredient			
				1	2	3	4					1	2	3	4
1.	Acute[1]	Oral						7.	Chronic[3]						
		Inhalation						8.	Fertility						
		Skin abs.						9.	Teratogenicity						
2.	Skin sensitisation							10.	Carcinogenicity						
3.	Skin irritation														
4.	Eye irritation							HUMAN DATA							
5.	Sub-acute[2]								Short-term						
6.	Mutagenicity								Long-term						

INGREDIENT 1 =   INGREDIENT 2 =
INGREDIENT 3 =   INGREDIENT 4 =

Notes: (1) Effects of a single dose; (2) Effects of repeated doses for 4-13 weeks; (3) Effects of repeated doses for 3-12 months.

6.
REFERENCES

The information shown in Sections 4 & 5 of this data sheet is drawn from the following sources:

9 Threshold limit values

To check that levels of a substance in the workroom air are properly controlled, you need to know its Threshold Limit Value (TLV). TLVs are limits designed to control levels of atmospheric contamination in the workplace.

There are TLVs for about 500 different substances. The TLVs are set by an American professional body called the American Conference of Governmental Industrial Hygienists (ACGIH) and their list is reprinted annually by the Health and Safety Executive for use in the UK. A small number of the TLVs are not accepted in the UK. Instead, the Health and Safety Commission issues its own 'control limits'.

TLV categories

There are several different forms of TLV:
1. **Ceiling limits.** These are limits which may not be exceeded at any time, even instantaneously. They have been set for a small number of fast-acting toxic substances.
2. **Time-weighted average** (TWA) **limits.** These are the limits used for most substances. The limits may be exceeded from time to time provided that the average exposure during an eight-hour day does not exceed the TLV.
3. **Short-term exposure limits** (STELS). These are maximum limits that may be reached – but not exceeded – on up to four occasions during the day for a maximum of 15 minutes at each time. There must be at least an hour between each exposure at this level.

A fuller explanation of these terms is given in the Health and Safety Executive's Guidance Note EH/15, which contains the TLV list. Useful explanations and examples are given in volume 7 of the Trades Union Congress coursebook for safety representatives *Chemical Hazards at Work.*

TLVs are not completely safe limits

The preface to the TLV list explains:
'Threshold limit values refer to airborne concentrations of substances and represent conditions under which it is believed that *nearly all workers may be repeatedly exposed day after day without adverse effect.* Because of wide variation in

individual susceptibility, however, a small percentage of workers may experience discomfort from some substances at concentrations at or below the threshold limit; *a smaller percentage may be affected more seriously by aggravation of a preexisting condition or by development of an occupational illness.'*

The HSE adds the following points:

'1. TLVs are not sharp dividing lines between "safe" and "dangerous" concentrations (but see special comments for substances with a "ceiling" (C) limit).

2. The best working practice is to reduce concentrations of all airborne contaminants as far below the TLV as is reasonably practicable. In the case of substances not quoted in the list or where there are no known toxic effects, exposure should be kept as low as is reasonably practicable.

3. The absence of a particular substance from the list does not necessarily indicate that it is "safe".'

Uneven protection

TLVs do not all give the same degree of protection. If you look at the TLVs shown in *Example 28* you will see that:

- TLVs often refer to completely different kinds of hazard. Some are short-term hazards, others are long-term. Some of the possible injuries are relatively minor, and reversible – others are serious and irreversible.
- Some have a built-in safety margin – others have none, and will undoubtedly allow injury to occur.

You cannot be sure you will avoid injury just by keeping concentrations below a TLV. In some cases, the TLV will protect you – in others a hazard may still exist. See *Example 29.*

You may sometimes be told that the TLV is the 'safe limit'. You should never treat any TLV as safe unless you positively know that (1) it takes into account *all* the known hazards of the substance concerned, and (2) it has an adequate margin of safety built-in. Even so, bear in mind the possibility that so-far undiscovered effects may exist.

You can find the evidence for individual TLVs in 'Documentation of the Threshold Limit Values' which is available from the American Conference of Governmental Industrial Hygienists, PO Box 1937, Cincinnati, Ohio 45201, USA.

Unless you have information to the contrary, it is probably best to think of TLVs as the concentrations at which exposure is

Example 28. **How much protection do TLVs give?**

The TLVs for different substances do not all give an equal degree of
protection. The aim of each of the TLVs below is described in the
words of the body that set them, the American Conference of
Governmental Industrial Hygienists, ('Documentation of the
Threshold Limit Values').

Some TLVs aim to prevent discomfort
Dibutyl phthalate 'recommended more from the standpoint of
controlling excessive airborne mists . . . rather than as a health
measure'
Propylene glycol monomethyl ether 'to avoid complaints from the
odour'

Other TLVs aim to prevent disabling disease
Methyl bromide 'to prevent serious neurotoxic effects and pulmonary
edema'
Octachloronaphthalene 'should prevent serious liver injury'

Some TLVs are set below levels known to cause injury to animals
Hexafluoroacetone 'definitely a "no-effect" level (in rats and dogs)'
Phenylphosphine 'would appear to have at least a 10-fold factor of
safety for mild, reversible changes in animals. Whether this limit
provides sufficient safety factor for exposed workers . , . will have to be
determined by human experience.'

Other TLVs have little or no safety margin
Quinone 'No systemic (affecting the whole body) effects . . . eye lesions
(injuries) are uncommon and mild when they do occur.'
Mica 'Should prevent disabling pneumoconiosis but may not be
sufficiently low to eliminate positive chest X-ray findings in workers
with many years' exposure.'
Monomethyl aniline 'offers very little margin of freedom from positive
blood findings'
Ozone 'may result in premature aging . . . if exposure is sufficiently
prolonged'
Phosphine 'does not take into account the possibility of chronic
phosphorous poisoning from phosphine'

Note: All TLVs cited are those in existence in 1979

probably harmful. This view is supported by the former Chief
Inspector of Factories who, in his 1973 report stated: 'Detection
of contamination approaching a TLV should always be regarded
as a sign that improved protection may be necessary.'
A good working rule is to use half the TLV as your standard.

• *Example 29.* **Irritating TLVs**

Irritation caused by fumes and vapours is not a trivial effect. The preface to the TLV list states: 'limits based on physical irritation should be considered no less binding than those based on physical impairment. There is increasing evidence that physical irritation may initiate, promote or accelerate physical impairment through interaction with other chemical or biologic agents.'

The 1979 TLVs for the substances below are shown alongside the concentrations known to cause irritation during an eight-hour exposure. **Note that some of the TLVs protect against irritation – but others do not.**

Substance	TLV (TWA) ppm	Irritating concentration (ppm) (for eight-hour exposure)	
Acetone	1,000	200 }	TLV permits
Ethyl acetate	400	100 }	irritation
Toluene	100	200 }	TLV prevents
Dioxane	50	200 }	irritation

Notes:
1. From 1981 it is proposed to change the TLV for acetone to 750 ppm and the TLV for dioxane to 25 ppm.
2. Data on irritation thresholds is drawn from: American Conference of Governmental Industrial Hygienists, *Industrial Ventilation: A Manual of Recommended Practice,* 14th ed., 1976.

Don't judge chemicals by their TLVs

Because individual TLVs have different objectives, you can't use them to decide which chemicals are safer than others. The preface to the TLV list specifically warns against this: 'TLVs are not intended for use, or for modification for use . . . as a relative indicator of hazard or toxicity'.

There are two reasons for this. Firstly, TLVs are set to deal with a variety of totally different hazards. One TLV may be set to prevent serious lung injury, another to avoid an unpleasant smell. Comparing the TLVs of the two wouldn't tell you which chemical was the more dangerous.

Secondly, TLVs are not set purely on medical grounds – they also take the costs of control into account. Many TLVs are not as low as they should be because the costs are judged too high. The most toxic substances do not necessarily have the lowest TLVs.

Example 30. **Substances with the same TLV may not be equally toxic**

Both trichloroethylene and propylene glycol monomethyl ether can cause narcosis. In 1979, both had the same TLV: 100 ppm TWA – although a reduction in the trichloroethylene limit had been proposed.

But although the two substances have the same TLV they are not equally dangerous. One causes ill-effects at one-tenth the TLV – the other is not hazardous until levels are ten times above the limit.

Trichloroethylene
'Workers exposed at concentrations averaging about 10 ppm (12 per cent of tests showed values above 40 ppm) showed slight to moderate pre-narcotic symptoms such as headache, dizziness and sleepiness. Persistent symptoms of an asthenic type (loss of strength) developed after months of exposure.'

Propylene glycol monomethyl ether
'Odour was transiently objectionable above 100 ppm. Higher concentrations were found to be more objectionable because of odor and lacrimation (watering of eyes) but evidence of anesthesia was not found until exposure approached 1000 ppm.'
Source: American Conference of Governmental Industrial Hygienists, 'Documentation of the Threshold Limit Values'.

Don't choose between chemicals on the basis of their TLVs. Substances with high TLVs are not necessarily safer than those with low TLVs – and substances with identical TLVs are not necessarily equally toxic. See *Example 30.*

TLVs and cancer

TLVs for carcinogens may reduce the risk but cannot guarantee freedom from a cancer hazard. At low doses, the human body can eliminate most chemicals without any ill-effects. If TLVs are set low enough, they can provide a safe working atmosphere.

However, as far as we know the body cannot handle even small doses of carcinogens safely. Even a tiny dose could lead to cancer, though the chance of this happening may be remote. The US National Institute for Occupational Safety and Health has stated: 'safe levels of exposure to carcinogens have not been demonstrated, but the possibility of cancer developing is lowered with decreasing exposure to carcinogens.'

This principle has been recognised by the HSC's Advisory Committee on Asbestos which in 1979 reported:

'We have failed ... to identify a threshold (for asbestos exposure) below which there is no evidence of adverse effects ... we believe it is inappropriate to continue to control exposure levels in terms of a "hygiene standard" as has been done hitherto. Such a concept is misleading in the case of asbestos as it implies a level of exposure below which exposure is safe.'

TLVs and suppliers' data sheets

Suppliers' data sheets may not always be a reliable source of information on TLVs. A survey by Social Audit in 1979 found that data sheets:

- Did not always inform users that a substance had a TLV.
- Occasionally quoted out-of-date TLVs or figures that were used overseas, but not in the UK.
- Sometimes failed to warn that some of the TLVs they quoted were 'ceiling' limits that should never be exceeded. If ceiling limits are used as TWA limits – which allow some excessive readings as long as the average concentration is within the limit – extremely dangerous conditions may occur.
- Rarely warned that some TLVs permit injury. *Example 31* suggests how this might be done.

Wherever possible, try to check any TLVs that are quoted to you, by consulting the TLV list (HSE Guidance Note EH/15). Check that the figures you use are accurate, up-to-date, and in the correct units – and that you distinguish between ceiling and TWA limits.

Volatility

Even if two substances were equally toxic – and had the same TLVs – their hazards could be quite different in practice. One might evaporate much faster than the other, producing dangerously high concentrations in a shorter time. The rate at which a liquid evaporates is called its 'volatility'.

Highly volatile liquids are much more likely to cause an inhalation hazard than liquids which evaporate slowly. A slow evaporating toxic liquid may be safer to use than a less toxic – but more volatile – alternative. You can tell how fast a liquid

Example 31. **Data sheets: TLVs**

An extract from a basic sheet is shown below. The full data sheet is shown on pages 79–82.

If the data sheet is properly completed, you should be told:

- **the TLV and its units**
- **what kind of TLV it is ('time-weighted average', 'ceiling', 'short-term exposure limit')**
- **its date (if it is more than a year old, check the latest TLV list to see if the figure has been changed)**
- **whether harmful effects are known to occur below the TLV.**

7.
EXPOSURE
LIMITS

THRESHOLD LIMIT VALUE (& units)					
SUBSTANCE	TWA	C	STEL	DATE	'Threshold limit values refer to airborne concentrations of substances and represent conditions under which it is believed that nearly all workers may be repeatedly exposed day after day without adverse effect. Because of wide variation in individual susceptibility, however, a small percentage of workers may experience discomfort from some substances at or below the threshold limit: a smaller percentage may be affected more seriously by aggravation of a pre-existing condition or by development of an occupational illness'. *(HSE Guidance Note EH 15)*

ILL-EFFECTS/DISCOMFORT BELOW TLV NOT KNOWN TO OCCUR ☐   DO OCCUR ☐
(Tick appropriate box; give brief details)

TLVs are revised periodically. For the latest figures and a full explanation of their use, see the most recent annual edition of HSE Guidance Note EH 15.

OTHER OCCUPATIONAL EXPOSURE LIMITS

evaporates by looking either at its boiling point or its 'vapour pressure'.

- The lower a liquid's boiling point is, the *faster* it evaporates.
- The lower a liquid's vapour pressure is, the *slower* it evaporates.

Note that all liquids evaporate more quickly as the temperature increases.

The vapour pressure is measured in units of 'millimetres of mercury', usually abbreviated to 'mm Hg'. The vapour pressure of a liquid increases with temperature, so it is normally measured at a standard temperature of 20°C or 25°C.

You may sometimes come across a third way of measuring volatility. This is the 'evaporation rate' – the speed at which the liquid evaporates compared to that of a standard solvent. Butyl

Example 32. **The volatility of some common liquids**

The table below shows the volatility of some common liquids measured in terms of both boiling point and vapour pressure.

	Boiling point (°C) lower = more volatile	*Vapour pressure* (mm Hg at 25°C) higher = more volatile
Acetone	56.2	226
1,1,1-Trichloroethane	74.0	125
Ethanol	78.5	50
Water	100.0	24
Mercury	356.6	0.012 (at 20°C)

acetate is often used as the standard solvent: its evaporation rate is taken as 1. A liquid that evaporates twice as fast as butyl acetate is said to have an evaporation rate of 2, and one that evaporates at half its speed an evaporation rate of 0.5.

There are two main reasons for needing to know the volatility of a liquid. (1) To design extraction systems that will be able to extract vapours from the air as fast as they evaporate into it, and (2) to reduce possible inhalation hazards by choosing the least volatile out of a range of equally toxic substances.

You can judge roughly how volatile a liquid is by comparing its boiling point or vapour pressure to that of one of the common liquids shown in *Example 32*.

10 Control measures

Most substances can be used safely if their hazards are understood and the right control measures used. These will usually aim to minimise exposure: but for some very toxic substances it may be necessary to prevent any exposure at all.

The Health and Safety Executive's advice
One problem – discussed in the previous section – is that we do

not always know the full hazards of a substance. For this reason, the Health and Safety Executive advises:

'It is therefore essential not only to exercise rigorous control measures for proven and suspected carcinogens but also to adopt a general precautionary policy for controlling the use of *all* substances, whether or not they are known to have any harmful effects.' (Guidance Note EH/18)

HSE Guidance Note EH/18 (*Toxic Substances: A Precautionary Policy*) lists the various control techniques that can be used:

'In most situations a combination of various control methods must be planned to provide adequate protection, with no single measure being relied upon exclusively:

a. *Substitution of less hazardous materials*
   this includes altering the synthesis routes to avoid using or producing toxic intermediates. Substitution may be required because the original material has been prohibited but in any case caution must be exercised, since use of a substitute not adequately tested could be as bad as, if not worse than, the original hazard

b. *Restriction of possible exposure*
   - minimise the number of, and restrict access to, essential personnel
   - limit the duration and degree of their exposure to within the TLV

c. *Segregation of plant and people*
   - total enclosure of process plant
   - physical separation with remote handling techniques

d. *Control of emissions from process:* so that a person's exposure is within the TLV
   - use of ventilation techniques, particularly local exhaust ventilation applied as near as possible to the source of emissions
   - wetting of dusty materials
   - pelleting
   - incorporation of toxic substances in 'master batches'
   - feeding of toxic substances to process in pre-packed containers.

e. *Personal protection:* various forms of protective clothing and respiratory protective equipment.
   The provision and use of personal protective equipment should normally be regarded as providing a back-up for other techniques which aim to control the risk at source,

rather than as a first line of defence; in certain circumstances however personal protection is the only reasonably practicable measure.

f. *General hygiene*
- application of 'good housekeeping' techniques such as use of vacuum cleaners with adequate filtration
- prohibition of eating and drinking in the workplace where toxic substances are used
- provision of good washing facilities to encourage a high standard of personal hygiene.

Whatever techniques are used, they should be subject to adequate checks on a regular basis to ensure that they are providing effective control. Where appropriate such checks should include regular sampling of the atmosphere, testing of the ventilation equipment, and servicing and maintenance of the protective equipment.'

Some of these measures have been referred to earlier in this book. See pages 12–15 for references to substitution of less harmful alternatives, ventilation, monitoring and the selection of protective equipment.

11 Emergency measures

In a sudden emergency, a supplier's data sheet may be the only source of information you can get to in time.

In the heat of the moment, there won't be time to phone around the workplace trying to discover who keeps the data sheets. So anyone likely to be involved (for example, first-aiders) should know in advance where they are kept.

Nor will there be time to hunt through a pile of reference books to check on a data sheet's information. If you have any doubts about a data sheet get it checked out *before* anything goes wrong.

Data sheets should tell you how to handle three types of emergency:
- overexposure
- spillages
- fire

• *Example 33.* **Data sheets: emergencies**

An extract from a basic data sheet is shown below. The full data sheet is shown on pages 79–82.

The data sheet should tell you how to deal with emergencies caused by:
- overexposure
- spillages
- fire

3.
EMERGENCY

OVEREXPOSURE		Note: if person is unconscious or having convulsions DO NOT attempt to cause vomiting or give liquids by mouth.
	EYES	
	SKIN	
	INHALED	
	SWALLOWED	
	INFORMATION FOR DOCTOR	

SPILL		
	CLEAN-UP METHOD	PROTECTIVE MEASURES
	DISPOSAL METHOD & STATUTORY CONTROLS	POTENTIAL ENVIRONMENTAL HAZARD

FIRE		
	UNUSUAL HAZARDS	COMBUSTION PRODUCTS & HAZARDS
	FIREFIGHTING PROCEDURES	
	EXTINGUISHER TYPE	

Note how this is done in *Example 33*. Data sheets should always give a phone number where you can reach the supplier in an emergency, day or night, if further information is needed.

Overexposure

The data sheet should tell you:
How to recognise signs of overexposure. Exposed workers should

be told of the symptoms caused by overexposure so that they can immediately recognise them and go for help if they are affected.

What first-aid treatment is required. Data sheets should tell you what first-aid treatment can be given while waiting for medical attention. First-aid advice should cover all the possible routes of exposure to the substance (inhaling, swallowing, skin or eye contact).

What special information a doctor may need. Doctors will know in general terms how to treat poisoning: but the specific treatment may depend on the chemical involved. In some cases the standard treatment may be ineffective or even dangerous; in others a specific antidote may exist (and should be kept on the premises – see *Example 34*). For this reason, a doctor will always need to know the *chemical composition* of any product involved in a case of over-exposure.

Spillage

Data sheets should tell you (1) the protective measures to use in case of a spillage, (2) the clean-up method, and (3) how to dispose of the waste.

Protective measures

After a large spillage, the fire or health hazard will generally be much greater than under normal conditions – so particularly stringent protective measures may be needed. People working near the spill area may be affected (and may even have to be evacuated), but the people most in need of special protection will be those actually involved in the clean-up.

Clean-up method

The clean-up method will depend on the physical form of the spilled substance.

- Dusts and gases may be removed from the air by exhaust ventilation. It may be dangerous to discharge highly toxic substances into the surrounding atmosphere, so these may have to be removed from the exhaust gas first.
- Spilled powders must be collected without spreading dust into the air. This may require 'damping down' with water sprays or the use of specially designed industrial vacuum cleaners.
- Liquids can be pumped out or absorbed into earth, sand or

Example 34. **The treatment of poisoning**

The extract below is taken from a data sheet on acrylonitrile. Note that it (1) gives first-aid advice, (2) contains specific guidance for doctors, and (3) recommends that the antidotes for acrylonitrile (one of the relatively few substances for which specific antidotes exist) be kept readily available.

'*Health Aspects*
Acrylonitrile is highly toxic . . . the lethal dose for an adult is less than 6 grammes and may be as low as 1 gramme. Works medical staff and local hospitals should be advised if acrylonitrile is being used so that emergency procedures are available for undertaking remedial therapy. It is recommended that first aid and medical kits containing the drugs and equipment necessary for emergency treatment by a doctor should be readily available at all locations where acrylonitrile exposure may occur.

First-aid kit should contain eyewash bottle, amyl nitrite capsules and instructions including casualty cards. Medical kit to contain Cobalt EDTA ampoules, syringes and needles . . .

Emergency treatment . . . Inhalation
Remove patient from exposure; keep warm and lying down. If respiratory distress is present, administer oxygen, break a capsule of amyl nitrite in a handkerchief and hold it about an inch from the patient's mouth and nostrils . . . Obtain medical assistance urgently . . .

Notes for medical officers
. . . the intravenous administration of 'Kelocyanor' (Cobalt EDTA) may prove beneficial . . .'

Source: Monsanto Europe, 'Acrylonitrile: Safety Aspects and Emergency Treatment'.

sawdust. In some cases, they may need to be treated with neutralising chemicals first.

Waste disposal
After they have been collected, some spilled substances may be reusable – but often they are contaminated and must be disposed of.

Because waste disposal can pollute the environment it requires special precautions – and these must comply with the pollution control laws.

Spilled liquids should not be washed into the drains unless the regional Water Authority has given its permission.

- *Example 35.* **Environmental damage caused by chemical spills**

The dangers of spilled chemicals are shown in the following incidents, reported by the Yorkshire Water Authority between 1978 and 1979. Note that many of these problems were caused when spilled chemicals were allowed to enter the drains.

'One hundred gallons of oil entered the stream via a surface water drain serving a smokeless fuel company . . . The oil contained a high proportion of toxic chemicals, and caused severe damage to the (plant and animal) life of the stream. **All fish life was extinguished for six miles and restrictions were imposed on the agricultural use of the stream . . .**'

'Wakefield Calder Vale Sewage Works was found to be affected by a discharge of acid. This was eventually found to be coming from the premises of (a chemical firm) where it was found that a pipe had been fractured and six tonnes of ammonium bisulphite had been lost to sewer. The result was that the sewage works treatment capacity had been destroyed, and **had workmen been working in the sewer at the time of the discharge a tragedy could have occurred . . .**'

'(Industrial waste) from a refuse tip at Bransholme containing high levels of ammonia **caused the death of at least 30,000 roach, perch, bream, pike and tench . . .**'

'A spillage of a very strong dye from a paper-making plant found its way to the River Don via a surface drain. Only 10 gallons of the dye was reported to have been lost but such was its intensity that **the river had the appearance of "port wine" for many miles . . .**'

Drains may discharge directly into rivers – and chemical spills may destroy river life or poison drinking water sources. Alternatively, the drains may lead to the sewage works, where spilled chemicals may create a fire hazard or affect the health of sewage workers. Even relatively harmless chemicals may react dangerously with other wastes once inside the sewage system.

The chemicals may also be toxic to the special bacteria used to treat sewage in sewage works. If a spilled substance interferes with the treatment process, raw sewage may be discharged into a river or coastline.

Tipping. Liquids and solids can be tipped on land – but only on approved and properly controlled sites. Otherwise liquid run-off from uncontrolled tipping can contaminate nearby rivers or underground water sources; unburied powders can be blown

Example 36. **Controlled waste disposal**

An extract from a data sheet on two related products is shown below.
Note that it:
- **warns of the hazards of disposal**
- **recommends disposal methods**
- **recommends standards for the quality of discharges**
- **urges consultation with the pollution authority.**

' "Penta" should not be allowed to pollute drains or waterways . . .
the Institution of Chemical Engineers recommends that all wastes
containing polychlorinated compounds should be incinerated. Since
"Penta" is a polychlorinated compound, we strongly urge that,
whenever practicable, this recommendation should be followed.
Since hydrogen chloride gas will be one of the products of
combustion, provision should be made for scrubbing and
neutralisation of the flue gases . . .'

'The disposal of aqueous solutions of "Santobrite" can often be
achieved by dilution and subsequent discharge through normal
effluent channels. The concentration of "Santobrite" which may be
discharged in this way should be established with the Effluent
Disposal Authority . . . where hazard to fish must be avoided, the
concentration of "Santobrite" should not exceed 0.01 ppm. Some
biological treatment plants . . . in particular those having an
anaerobic sludge digestion stage may require the level of
pentachlorophenates to be less than 0.4 ppm.'

Source: Monsanto Europe, 'Santobrite and Monsanto Penta'.

around the neighbourhood, and chemicals may react together
on a tip giving off poisonous fumes.

Incineration. Certain chemicals can be burned without producing toxic products – they can sometimes be safely burned in the
works boiler and actually save fuel. Other substances give off
toxic gases when burned and should only be handled in specially
designed incinerators, with proper pollution controls.

Some of the effects of poor waste disposal are shown in *Example
35. Example 36* shows a data sheet which recommends specific
waste disposal methods.

Fire

Data sheets should tell you what fire risk a substance presents,
and how to deal with a fire if one occurs.

The fire hazard

The flash point is the key to a flammable liquid's fire hazard. In a fire, it is the *vapour* evaporating from a flammable liquid which burns – not the liquid itself. A spark or flame will only set fire to this vapour if there is enough of it in the air.

At low temperatures, a liquid may evaporate too slowly to produce a flammable mixture with air. As the temperature increases the rate of evaporation goes up and a flammable mixture may be produced.

The temperature at which the liquid gives off enough vapour to catch fire if ignited is called its 'flash point' (f.p.). If the flash point of a liquid is lower than the surrounding temperature, a fire hazard will exist.

Petrol (f.p. −43°C), acetone (f.p. −18°C) and ethyl alcohol (f.p. 13°C) all have flash points below normal room temperature – and all are therefore serious fire hazards. Castor oil (f.p. 230°C) and paraffin wax (f.p. 199°C) will not present a fire hazard at room temperature – but would become dangerous if used at high temperatures.

Combustion products

Substances may give off highly toxic gases when they burn – even though they themselves are relatively innocuous. Burning polyurethane foam releases deadly hydrogen cyanide; PVC may give off hydrochloric acid. Data sheets should identify any specially toxic or unusual 'combustion products'.

Fire extinguishers

A range of different fire extinguishing materials exist including water, carbon dioxide, foam, chemical powders, and the so-called 'vaporising liquids'. For some fires, almost any extinguisher will do – but in other cases using the wrong extinguisher can be dangerous.

For example, although water is in general the most effective extinguisher, it can cause a violent explosion if used on burning metals or oxidising substances. If it is used on flammable liquids that are lighter than water these may float on top of the water and spread the fire. Data sheets should therefore specify which extinguishing materials can be used in case of fire.

In the UK, liquids with a flash point below 32°C must be labelled 'highly flammable'. (32°C is taken as the maximum outdoor shade temperature likely to occur in the UK.)

Data sheets will normally tell you whether a liquid is flammable, and give you its flash point. The method used to determine the flash point ('open cup' or 'closed cup' method) may also be given. These give slightly different readings, but unless very precise figures are needed the difference is not significant.

Two other figures also give information about the fire risk:

The flammable limits. These are the maximum and minimum proportions of vapour in air that will provide a flammable mixture. Below the lower flammable limit, the mixture contains too little vapour to burn – above the upper limit the mixture is too rich to burn. The flammable limits are sometimes also described as the 'explosive limits'.

The auto-ignition temperature. This is the temperature at which a substance will catch fire without coming into contact with a flame or spark. Contact with a hot surface, for example, would be enough to start a fire. Carbon disulphide, for example, has an auto-ignition temperature of 100°C and would catch fire if splashed onto a pipe carrying steam.

12 Using data sheets

Your employers can only provide a safe workplace if they know the hazards of all the chemicals used – and make sure that those who handle them do too. If you are a safety representative, you should try to ensure that your employer obtains all the necessary information – and acts on it.

What your employer should do

List chemicals

Ask your employer to prepare a complete list of all substances used in the workplace. The list should cover *all* substances used – not just those someone classifies as 'hazardous'. It should say where each substance is used, and for what purpose.

Without this list you will never have a full picture of the hazards in the workplace. The list will make it possible to:

- Systematically survey hazards and precautions throughout the workplace. If you need to, you can then single out certain problems for priority attention.
- Immediately respond to reports of new hazards. If you have a list of all the chemicals you use you can immediately tell whether the chemical involved is used in the workplace and decide whether new precautions may be needed.

If you are a safety representative, you have a right to all relevant health and safety information in your employer's possession – and this includes information about which chemicals are used.

Record exposures

Ask your employer to keep a comprehensive record of every employee's exposure to chemicals. The hazards of some of the chemicals now used will only be discovered in the future. Exposure records may be the only way of identifying those workers who have been exposed in the past so that:

- a suspected health hazard can be fully investigated
- people at risk can be sent for medical check-ups
- compensation can be obtained.

Records should give the name of every chemical to which the employee has been exposed, its use and the period of exposure. They should also describe any protective equipment worn, the results of any air monitoring, and details of any illnesses that may have occurred at the time. Because occupational illnesses may only develop some years after exposure began, these records should be retained after an employee has left the job or retired. Guidance on record-keeping is given in HSE Guidance Note MS/18 – 'Health Surveillance by Routine Procedures'.

Collect data sheets

Get your employer to obtain full supplier's information on every substance used. Don't ignore data sheets until a specific problem comes up. It can easily be several weeks before you get all the information you need out of a supplier. Data sheets should be collected in advance so that users can take proper precautions *before* a problem occurs. See *Example 37.*

Check data sheets

Your employer should make sure that there are no major gaps in the suppliers' data sheets. One of the most important items of information is the chemical composition of the product. Without

Example 37. **Data sheets should be obtained in advance – even if no problem is suspected**

'Airflow Streamlines Ltd of Northampton were fined £300 on a neglect of safety charge after a worker was burned while opening a drum of corrosive paint stripper.

Northampton Magistrates' Court heard that four employees were not wearing protective clothing when they opened the drum. One of them, Mr Peter Hollowell, was splashed on the hands, face and chest, leaving him burned and in terrible pain, the bench was told.

The accident happened as Mr Hollowell was attempting to open the drum which was very tight. Corrosive liquid came out of the hole with a "whoosh" and it splashed over his hands, face and chest. "He fell and cut his head while trying to get his sodden overalls off – the liquid was burning him and he was in terrible pain" said the factory inspector.

The company admitted not ensuring the safety of four employees by not instructing them on how to open the drum . . . Defending the company, Mr Bernard Singleton said they did not know about the danger . . . *The day AFTER the accident they had received a warning letter about this from the manufacturers.'*

Source: *Northampton Chronicle & Echo,* 14 February 1981.

this, neither your employer nor you can ever be sure that you are using the right safety precautions. Pages 21–25 suggest what to do if you have trouble discovering the chemical composition of a product.

The *Checklist* on pages 83–85 shows the other areas of information that the data sheet should cover.

Your employer should cross-check suppliers' information with other sources before using it. Suppliers' information can be very helpful and may be essential – particularly if unusual hazards or specialised precautions are involved.

But suppliers' information is not always wholly reliable. Data sheets sometimes give incomplete or inaccurate information (see pages 18–19). The size or reputation of the supplier does not always guarantee the quality of the information.

Employers cannot excuse themselves of their duty to provide a safe workplace by complaining that suppliers provide poor information. Suppliers' data sheets are only one of the sources of information the employer should consult. They should be used with – and not as a substitute for – information from independent sources.

Your employer should inform suppliers of any mistakes found in their data sheets. They can then correct the errors and if necessary notify other customers of serious mistakes. In this way, your employer's checking will also help other users.

If the error is serious, the Health and Safety Executive should be told – and the supplier informed that this is being done. Some suppliers may repeatedly make mistakes – or be unwilling to correct data sheets. They are more likely to take action if they know the HSE has been informed.

Reject products with inadequate information

Your employer's policy should be to refuse to use substances if suppliers' information is inadequate. An inadequate data sheet doesn't matter if you can get all the missing information from reference books. If you can't, your employer should warn uncooperative suppliers that unless information is provided the products will no longer be used. If they still refuse, your employer should look for alternative products which *are* accompanied by proper information.

What you should do

Get access to data sheets

Make sure you have full access to all suppliers' data sheets received by your employer. Your right to this information is specifically laid down in the Code of Practice on Safety Representatives – see page 92.

If you do not get this information directly there are several things you can do:

1. Contact your company doctor. If you have a company doctor, he or she should act as an independent professional adviser, rather than as a part of management. The Royal College of Physicians has given specific advice to company doctors on their duty to protect the health of employees by providing information:

'Normally the employer will disclose (health and safety) information and should such confidential information concerning the injurious nature of a new process or product come into the possession of the occupational physician he should remind the employer of his responsibilities . . . if the management of the organisation refuse permission for such specific disclosure . . . *his (the doctor's) responsibility for workers exposed to hazards should take precedence over the management's refusal to disclose.'* Royal College of Physicians, Faculty of Occupational Medicine. 'Guidance on Ethics for Occupational Physicians', 1980.

2. Complain to the factory inspector. The factory inspector should ensure that your employer carries out their legal obligation to provide you with information. If an inspector accepts that your complaint is justified he or she should tell your employer to provide the information – or may even give it to you directly.

3. Write to individual suppliers yourself. A letter which you can use to do this is shown in *Example 38*. If this doesn't get you all the information you need, it may be worth writing again sending a copy of the data sheet shown on pages 79–82 and asking the supplier to complete it.

The *Checklist* on pages 83–85 shows what information suppliers should provide. If you have already got much of this information just ask the supplier to complete those sections of the blank data sheet not covered by their original information. Don't worry about asking for more information than you can use yourself. Your union's health and safety officer will often be able to interpret the information for you.

4. Ask your union to write to suppliers. Not all suppliers answer requests for information from safety representatives. If you don't get a satisfactory reply, you can ask your union's health and safety – or other – officer to write on your behalf. If you do, it will help your union officer if you:

- identify the product as fully as you can
- explain what it is used for
- give the full name and address of the supplier
- send any other information about the product that you already have.

5. Refuse to handle the product. If you are denied access to data sheets and proper information about products you use, you may want to consider advising your members not to work with the substances concerned.

Check safety precautions

Use suppliers' data sheets to check that your safety precautions and the warnings given to workers are adequate. If they are not, then new precautions or warnings will be needed.

If the information on a data sheet has not been acted on, this may be a sign of a wider problem. Data sheets may not be

● *Example 38.* **Standard letter to suppliers**

If you are unable to obtain suppliers' information from your employer you may want to write directly to the supplier (see page 71). You can use the standard letter shown below to do this.

The Sales Manager
Company name and address   *date*

Dear Sir or Madam,

I am writing to ask if you can supply me with health and safety information about one of your products: *(give full name of product).*

I understand that, as required by section 6(4) of the Health and Safety at Work Act 1974, you maintain information about the hazards of this substance and any measures needed to ensure that the product can be used safely.

I am a trade union safety representative whose members work with this product, and would be grateful if you could supply me with your full health and safety information on this product, including:

1. The chemical names of all the ingredients present and an approximate indication of their proportions.

2. Details of the potential harmful effects caused by over-exposure to each ingredient, including long-term as well as short-term hazards, by all routes of exposure.

3. The precautions needed to ensure that the product can be used without risks to health.

Any information you supply will be used for health and safety purposes only and will not be used or divulged for any other reason.

I shall appreciate your help with this enquiry and look forward to hearing from you.

Yours sincerely,

Your name

getting through to the right people in management – or they may be being ignored. This can only be put right if your employer develops a systematic and effective system for collecting and using health and safety information.

Check data sheets
You may want to check the accuracy of some data sheets yourself. It is possible that your employer is following the supplier's advice – but the advice is itself inadequate.

It is only worth checking the accuracy of data sheets if your employer acts on them. If your employer ignores suppliers' data sheets and only uses information from a trade association, then check the trade association's advice – not the supplier's. If your employer produces special information for internal use – check this information. In either case, suppliers' information should still be available and may help in your checking.

You may use too many different substances to hope to check every data sheet. Your aim should be to check a sample. You may decide to choose these because:

- People who handle the substances complain of discomfort or illness – and you want to make sure that the supplier is recommending the correct safety precautions.
- New hazards have recently been reported and you want to know if the supplier took these into account in the data sheet.
- You use many chemicals from the same supplier and want to know if the supplier's information is reliable.

Pages 74–78 give advice on how to check data sheets using reference books.

If a data sheet contains errors this may mean that your safety precautions are inadequate. It may also mean that your employer is not checking suppliers' information before acting on it – so there may be undetected errors in other data sheets too. Your employer should systematically evaluate *all* the suppliers' information they have acted on so that they can detect any other mistakes that may have been made.

Work with your union
Use your union's facilities – and keep the union informed of your progress. If your union has a health and safety officer, he or she may be able to give you a lot of help with chemical problems. But see if you can help yourself before contacting the officer. If you have access to health and safety reference books you may be able to get the information you need directly. If you can't, or if

you need help interpreting what you find, your health and safety officer can often give you specialist advice.

Your own experiences may also be helpful to other safety representatives – so keep your union informed about any significant progress you make. Let them know if you:

- Detect errors in a supplier's data sheet. Your health and safety officer may be able to build up a picture of which suppliers are producing unreliable information – and either press them to improve their data sheets or ask the HSE to take action.
- Come across any particularly helpful suppliers – for example those that are prepared to reveal the chemical composition of trade-named products. Other safety representatives may want to ask their employers to use products from suppliers known to have good disclosure policies.
- Reach any significant safety or disclosure of information agreements. These can serve as a model for safety representatives in other establishments.
- Discover any new sources of information or help. The health and safety officer may want to recommend these to other safety representatives.

13 Investigating chemicals

Finding reference books

There is no single book that will give you full information on the hazards of all the substances you may use. It is usually worth looking a substance up in several different sources, if necessary taking bits of information from each.

A list of the most useful books is given on pages 85–89.

Your employer should be using at least some of these books. If so, your employer should give you access to them as well. See page 92.

If you can't get these books at work you should be able to find some of them in a good reference library or get permission to use them at a local polytechnic or university library. If your library doesn't have them, ask the library to borrow them for you from another library. It may even buy them if it feels they will be used regularly.

Wherever possible, use the most up-to-date sources available. The amount of information known about toxic substances is increasing all the time – so reference books can become out-of-date very quickly. The 1977 edition of one list of toxic chemicals contained information on some 10,000 substances not mentioned in the 1975 edition. The more recent the sources of information you use, the better are your chances of learning about recent discoveries.

Looking the substance up

To check a data sheet, all you have to do is look up the substance in a reference source and see if it adds to or contradicts the data sheet. See how this has been done in *Examples 13, 18* and *19.*

You cannot look a substance up by its trade name – you must know its proper chemical name. Reference books don't list substances by suppliers' trade-names. So to check a data sheet you must know the product's chemical composition. This is one reason why you should try to get unidentified trade-named substances banned from your workplace.

If you are investigating the hazards of a mixture, look up each ingredient separately. Some mixtures may have additional hazards to those of the individual ingredients – but these are rarely studied. You will normally only be able to find information about the individual ingredients – not about the effects of the mixture as a whole.

Getting the chemical name right

Be careful not to confuse your substance with another of similar name. Completely different substances often have names which differ from each other by only a single letter. For example, arsenate and arsenite, sulphide and sulphite, benzene and benzine.

A second problem is that the same substance is sometimes known by several alternative names or 'synonyms'. For example, ethyl acetate is also called acetic ether, ethyl acetic ester and ethyl ethanoate.

Begin your search by writing down all the different names of the substance you come across. (Chemical dictionaries and some of the main reference books will list these.) Then if you can't find the substance in the index of the book you are using, check to see if it is listed under one of its alternative names.

If you find a substance with a similar but not identical name to the one you are investigating, check (1) its synonyms, and (2) its chemical formula.

The chemical formula is a set of letters and numbers showing the types and numbers of atoms that make up a basic unit of the substance.

If two chemical names refer to the same substance, you will find that:
- both have the same chemical formula, and
- when you look one of the names up, the other name will be listed as a 'synonym' – an alternative name.

See *Example 39.*

Sometimes different substances share the same chemical formulae – but if they do, they always have different synonyms. When this happens, the two related substances (which are called *'isomers'*) are sometimes distinguished from each other by having different numbers or Greek letters such as 'alpha' or 'beta' in or before the name. Never overlook numbers or letters in a chemical name: they are a vital part of it. Isomers may have different toxic properties from each other, so it is important not to mix them up.

Medical jargon

Don't be discouraged if you come across medical jargon: often it can be easily translated into ordinary language. Every job – not just medicine – has its own jargon. Your job almost certainly has special words for describing the tools, equipment, operations or parts of the workplace you use. These terms would probably seem as strange to a doctor as medical terms do to you. Most of it can be cleared up by a simple explanation.

If you receive a data sheet with unfamiliar medical terms, ask your employer to explain them. If necessary an employer can always get the information for you from the company doctor. Alternatively, you may find that your own GP can be a useful source of information.

You can look medical terms up for yourself with the help of a pocket medical dictionary. Some medical dictionaries use very technical language, so it is worth looking around to find one that suits you. Two useful and inexpensive publications are:

Example 39. **How to tell substances with similar names apart**

If you are investigating the hazards of TOLUENE you may come across two substances with similar names, TOLUOL and O-TOLUIDINE.

	TOLUENE	*TOLUOL*	*O-TOLUIDINE*
Alternative names ('synonyms')	*Methyl benzene* *Phenyl methane* *Toluol* *Methyl benzol*	*Toluene*	*2-Amino-1-methyl benzene* *Amino toluene* *2-Methyl aniline*
Formula	$C_6H_5CH_3$	$C_6H_5CH_3$	$C_6H_4CH_3NH_2$

Checking the synonyms and formulae of these shows that TOLUENE and TOLUOL are two names for the same substance. Each name is listed as a synonym of the other, and the two have the same chemical formula. O-TOLUIDINE, however, is completely unrelated.

If you are investigating the hazards of 1,1,1,-TRICHLOROETHANE you may come across a substance with an almost identical name, 1,1,2-TRICHLOROETHANE.

	1,1,1,-Trichloroethane	1,1,2-Trichloroethane
Alternative names ('synonyms')	*Methyl chloroform* *Alpha-trichloroethane*	*Ethane trichloride* *Vinyl trichloride* *Beta-trichloroethane*
Formula	$C_2H_3Cl_3$	$C_2H_3Cl_3$

The two names refer to ISOMERS – different substances which share the same formula. Note that there are no common synonyms. The two substances have different toxic properties (1,1,2-TRI-CHLOROETHANE is considerably more toxic than 1,1,1,-TRI-CHLOROETHANE) and different TLVs.

Pocket Medical Dictionary or *Nurses Dictionary,* edited by Nancy Roper, Churchill Livingstone, £1.20. These two dictionaries are virtually identical – either one will do.
The Penguin Medical Encyclopaedia, Peter Wingate, Penguin, £1.95.

If you don't succeed . . .

Don't be surprised if some of your efforts to get information on chemicals are unsuccessful. It can be very difficult to get hold of all the information you need – so don't be discouraged. Even the most experienced researchers sometimes draw a complete blank. There may be two reasons for this:

- *The standard reference books only cover the commoner substances.* Information on other substances, or findings made in the last two or three years, may be published in scientific journals but not have reached the reference books yet. Your union's health and safety or research officer may be able to locate these articles for you by doing a computer search or going through an abstracts journal (see page 87).

- *Little or nothing may be known about the hazards of the substance.* There are more than four million different known chemicals. The most comprehensive list of tested chemicals contained information on only 39,000 of these in 1979 – and in most cases the information available was absolutely minimal. In some cases, a manufacturer may have tested a product – but not published the results. So it may be impossible to check the information on the manufacturer's data sheet.

If you don't get the information you need from reference sources, pass the query on to your union's health and safety or research department – and give them any information you already have (see page 71). In some cases you may find that the Factory Inspectorate or a local health and safety group can also help with queries.

At times no-one will be able to discover any information on the chemical – but this doesn't mean it is safe. **Never regard a substance as safe just because its hazards are not known or are not mentioned in the books you consult.**

A recommended data sheet

HEALTH AND SAFETY INFORMATION

1.
IDENTIFICATION

| PRODUCT NAME | APPEARANCE |
| | ODOUR |

| SUPPLIER'S NAME & ADDRESS | EMERGENCY PHONE NO. (Day/Night/Weekend) |
| | ASK FOR |

IMPORTANT: If any section of this form is not relevant or cannot be completed, the supplier should enter one of the following phrases: 'No Data', 'None/No Hazard', 'Not Applicable for following reason. . .'. If a box has been left blank, the user should check with the supplier to ensure that no oversight has occurred.

2.
COMPOSITION

	CHEMICAL NAMES & SYNONYMS	FORMULAE	APPROXIMATE PROPORTIONS
INGREDIENTS			
IMPURITIES			

All ingredients should be listed. Generalisations such as 'hydrocarbons', 'alcohols', 'chlorinated solvents' are not sufficient. Proper chemical names and formulae are essential for evaluating toxicity.

3.
EMERGENCY

OVEREXPOSURE

EYES		Note: if person is unconscious or having convulsions DO NOT attempt to cause vomiting or give liquids by mouth.
SKIN		
INHALED		
SWALLOWED		
INFORMATION FOR DOCTOR		

SPILL

| CLEAN-UP METHOD | PROTECTIVE MEASURES |
| DISPOSAL METHOD & STATUTORY CONTROLS | POTENTIAL ENVIRONMENTAL HAZARD |

FIRE

UNUSUAL HAZARDS	COMBUSTION PRODUCTS & HAZARDS
FIREFIGHTING PROCEDURES	
EXTINGUISHER TYPE	

4.
HEALTH HAZARD

	EFFECTS OF SHORT-TERM EXPOSURE for each ingredient	EFFECTS OF LONG-TERM EXPOSURE for each ingredient	1ST DETECTABLE SIGNS OF OVEREXPOSURE Important: the absence of these signs does not necessarily mean conditions are safe!
	Wherever possible, the minimum concentration/exposure period thought to be capable of producing ill-effects should be specified.		
IF INHALED			
IF SWALLOWED			
IF ABSORBED THROUGH SKIN			
ON SKIN			
IN EYE			
	'NO HAZARD KNOWN' indicates that the substance has been tested and no hazard found. 'NO INFORMATION' indicates that the substance has not been tested. It should be treated as hazardous.		

5.
EXTENT OF TESTING

The table below shows which toxicity tests have been carried out on the product and/or its individual ingredients. The tests listed are those that will be required for new chemicals under the proposed Notification of New Substances Regulations. Tests 1-6 will be required for all new substances. For some substances, Tests 7-10 may also be required.

Where a particular test has been carried out on the product or an individual ingredient, a cross should be entered in the appropriate box. A cross merely indicates that a test has been carried out: it does not describe the results of the test.

ANIMAL DATA		Pro-duct	Ingredient 1	2	3	4			Pro-duct	Ingredient 1	2	3	4
1. Acute[1]	Oral						7. Chronic[3]						
	Inhalation						8. Fertility						
	Skin abs.						9. Teratogenicity						
2. Skin sensitisation							10. Carcinogenicity						
3. Skin irritation													
4. Eye irritation							HUMAN DATA						
5. Sub-acute[2]							Short-term						
6. Mutagenicity							Long-term						

INGREDIENT 1 =
INGREDIENT 3 =

INGREDIENT 2 =
INGREDIENT 4 =

Notes: (1) Effects of a single dose; (2) Effects of repeated doses for 4-13 weeks; (3) Effects of repeated doses for 3-12 months.

6.
REFERENCES

The information shown in Sections 4 & 5 of this data sheet is drawn from the following sources:

7. EXPOSURE LIMITS

THRESHOLD LIMIT VALUE (& units)					
SUBSTANCE	TWA	C·	STEL	DATE	

"Threshold limit values refer to airborne concentrations of substances and represent conditions under which it is believed that nearly all workers may be repeatedly exposed day after day without adverse effect. Because of wide variation in individual susceptibility, however, a small percentage of workers may experience discomfort from some substances at or below the threshold limit; a smaller percentage may be affected more seriously by aggravation of a pre-existing condition or by development of an occupational illness'. *(HSE Guidance Note EH 15)*

ILL-EFFECTS/DISCOMFORT BELOW TLV NOT KNOWN TO OCCUR ☐ DO OCCUR ☐
(Tick appropriate box; give brief details)

TLVs are revised periodically. For the latest figures and a full explanation of their use, see the most recent annual edition of HSE Guidance Note EH 15.

OTHER OCCUPATIONAL EXPOSURE LIMITS

8. LEGAL REQUIREMENTS

THE FOLLOWING REGULATIONS & STATUTES APPLY

9. CONTROL MEASURES

MEASURES OTHER THAN PERSONAL PROTECTION

NOTES BY HSE: (1) 'The best working practice is to reduce concentrations of all airborne contaminants as far below the TLV as is reasonably practicable. In the case of substances not quoted on the (TLV) list or where there are no known toxic effects exposures should be kept as low as practicable'. (2) 'Whatever techniques are used, they should be subject to adequate checks on a regular basis to ensure that they are providing effective control'.   (3) 'Where the atmosphere of a workplace is likely to be contaminated, analysis of the atmosphere should be carried out on a periodic basis'.
(HSE Guidance Notes EH 15 and EH 18)

10. PERSONAL PROTECTION

INHALATION

EYES

HANDS,FACE,BODY

SPECIAL ITEMS TO BE KEPT IN 1ST AID BOX

NOTE BY HSE. 'The provision and use of personal protective equipment should normally be regarded as providing a back-up for other techniques which aim to control the risk at source, rather than as a first line of defence; in certain circumstances however personal protection is the only reasonably practicable measure'. *(Guidance Note EH 18)*

11. STORAGE

STORAGE & HANDLING MEASURES

SPECIAL CONTAINER DESIGN & MATERIALS

DECOMPOSITION PRODUCTS & HAZARDS	CONDITIONS LEADING TO DECOMPOSITION
POLYMERISATION PRODUCTS & HAZARDS	CONDITIONS LEADING TO POLYMERISATION
INCOMPATIBLE SUBSTANCES & HAZARDS	

12. FIRE DATA

SPECIAL PRECAUTIONS		
FLASH POINT & METHOD	AUTOIGNITION TEMPERATURE	FLAMMABLE LIMITS (%)
		Lower Upper

13. PHYSICAL DATA

BOILING POINT	VAPOUR PRESSURE	SPECIFIC GRAVITY
VAPOUR DENSITY	MELTING/ FREEZING PT	% VOLATILES

Note: If any of the above data refer to individual ingredients and not to the whole product, this should be indicated.

14. INFORMATION

1. This data sheet contains information that could save lives in an emergency. Those likely to be involved in any emergency should:

   o be familiar with the contents of this data sheet

   o know where it is kept

   o have immediate access to it at all times

   It may be helpful to display information from this data sheet on wall placards in the area where the product is used.

2. Everyone likely to come in contact with the product should:

   o be informed of any possible hazard

   o be familiar with the necessary safety measures and understand the consequences of ignoring them

   o be familiar with the symptoms that may develop from overexposure

   o be urged to report any health abnormality, however trivial.

3. Copies of this data sheet should be made available to trade union safety representatives. (*Code of Practice on Safety Representatives, paragraph 6 (b). HMSO, 1977.*)

4. If this product is transferred from its original container to a new one, the new container should be labelled with the name of the product and the following information:

HAZCHEM NO.	UN NO.

5. Other publications containing information on the safe use of this product include:

This information is believed to be accurate and up-to-date at the time of issue. However, new information may subsequently have come to light. Users should check with the supplier periodically to confirm that the data sheet remains up-to-date.

PREPARED BY	POSITION
SIGNATURE	DATE

© Social Audit Ltd 1981

Full size (A4) blank copies of this data sheet may be obtained from Social Audit, 9 Poland Street, London W1V 3DG. Price 50p each, post-free.

Checklist on suppliers' information

This checklist tells you what should be covered by suppliers' health and safety information.

Composition
1. The chemical names of all ingredients in the product – not just the trade name.
2. Details of any impurities.
3. Approximate proportions of each ingredient and any impurity present.

Exposure routes
4. Possible hazard by all likely routes of exposure. Depending on the substance and its physical form, these may include:
   (a) inhaling
   (b) swallowing
   (c) skin absorption
   (d) eye contact
   (e) skin contact

Potential injury
5. The hazards of each ingredient.
6. Early symptoms of overexposure.
7. Consequences of severe overexposure.
8. Concentration and period of exposure causing injury.

Long-term hazard
9. The effects of long-term as well as short-term exposure.
10. Where no long-term hazard is described, is it clear whether this is because no hazard exists – or because no research has been done?

Evidence
11. Evidence for any opinions about the hazard (e.g. 'little hazard', 'not generally regarded as toxic').
12. References to sources of hazard information consulted by supplier.

Control methods
13. Measures needed to prevent contamination of the workplace and remove any contamination (e.g. by ventilation) that does occur.

Personal Protection
14. Protective equipment needed for (a) skin (b) eyes (c) inhalation.

Exposure limits
15. Any exposure limits (such as TLVs) that may apply.

First aid
16. First aid measures to use in case of (a) inhaling (b) swallowing (c) eye splashes (d) skin contamination.
17. Any special information needed by doctors treating cases of poisoning.

Fire
18. The flash point (for flammable liquids).
19. Any special hazards (e.g. from combustion products) and fire-fighting measures needed.
20. Extinguisher type.

Spills
21. Clean-up method.
22. Protective measures for those dealing with the spill.
23. Disposal method which avoids environmental hazard.

Chemical reactions
24. Whether the substance can decompose, and if so:
    (a) under what conditions
    (b) what hazards result
    (c) what preventive measures are needed
25. Whether the substance reacts with other chemicals, and if so:
    (a) which chemicals
    (b) what hazards may result

Storage
26. Any special precautions needed for the (a) storage (b) transport or (c) handling of the product.

Phone
27. Emergency phone number that can be used, day or night, to contact the supplier if further information is needed.

Date
28. Date when the information was prepared (so you can tell if it is likely to include recent findings).

Sources of information on chemical hazards

Encyclopaedia of Occupational Health and Safety. International Labour Office, 96–98 Marsham Street, London SW1, 2 vols, 1972 edition. Out of print at time of writing. New edition not expected before 1983. One of the most useful books you will find, with articles on the hazards of chemicals, control techniques, occupational diseases and many other subjects. The 1972 edition does not contain recent information on chemicals, but is still valuable.

Documentation of the Threshold Limit Values. American Conference of Governmental Industrial Hygienists, PO Box 19367, Cincinnati, Ohio, 45201, USA. This shows the evidence on which the TLVs for some 500 different substances have been set. If the substance you are looking up has a TLV, this is the best source of information on its hazards. Essential reading if you want to know how much protection any individual TLV is expected to give.

Dangerous Properties of Industrial Materials. N. I. Sax. Van Nostrand Reinhold, New York, 5th edition, 1979. Contains information on some 15,000 chemicals – far more than any of the other standard reference books. Many of the entries are extremely brief – but this may be the only easily available source of information on the hazards of less common chemicals.

Patty's Industrial Hygiene and Toxicology. Published by John Wiley and Sons, New York, 3 vols. Vol. 1. 'General Principles' (1978); vol. 2. 'Toxicology', published in three parts: the first appeared in 1981, the remaining two were unpublished at the time of going to print; vol. 3. 'Theory and Rationale of Industrial Hygiene Practice' (1979).

Reactive Chemical Hazards. Ed. L. Bretherick, Royal Society of Chemistry, London, 3rd edition, 1980, £15. This tells you which chemicals a substance reacts dangerously with – and what reaction products result.

Occupational Diseases: A Guide to their Recognition. National Institute for Occupational Safety and Health, US Department of Health, Education and Welfare. US Government Printing Office, June 1977. Useful summaries of the hazards, and recommended safety precautions, for some of the commoner chemicals.

Environmental and Industrial Health Hazards: A Practical Guide. R. A. Trevethick, London, William Heinemann Medical Books, 1976, £5.75. A clearly written book which uses non-technical language – but which covers only a hundred of the commoner substances.

Work is Dangerous to Your Health. J. M. Stellman & S. M. Daum, New York, Vintage Books, 1973. (Available from BSSRS, 9 Poland Street, London W1V 3DG, £2.40.) A clear guide to the hazards of commoner chemicals, written as a workers' reference book.

Social Audit Pollution Handbook: How to Assess Environmental and Workplace Pollution. Maurice Frankel, London, Macmillan, 1978. (Available from Social Audit, 9 Poland Street, London W1V 3DG, £3.95.) A guide to using information to evaluate air and water pollution hazards from industry. The approach is similar to the one used in this guide.

Health and Safety Executive Publications Catalogue. London, HMSO, 1980 edition, £3.50. An up-to-date alphabetical index of all HSE and HSC publications. The best way of finding out whether the substance you are interested in is covered by official publications or regulations.

The Hazards of Work: A Workers' Guide to Health and Safety at Work. Patrick Kinnersly, London, Pluto, 1973. An essential introduction to workplace hazards with very brief information on many individual chemicals.

For latest information

Hazards Bulletin. Work Hazards Group, 3 Surrey Place, Sheffield S1 2LP, £2.10 a year for five issues. News and summaries of recent information about individual chemicals.

CIS Abstracts. International Labour Office, 96–98 Marsham Street, London SW1. A magazine made up entirely of summaries of new articles or reports on health and safety. Look your chemical up in the annual index for references to articles published during the year, then look at the summaries of any relevant papers. Can be used to get up-to-date information on any substance. Particularly helpful if your reference books are a few years old.

Toxline Computer Searches. Available from the British Library, Medlars Section, Boston Spa, Wetherby, West Yorks. Tel. 0937-843434. One of several computerised sources of information. These provide an easy, but expensive, way of discovering recent information about a chemical. For £25 + VAT you get references to, and summaries of, publications about your chemical. HSELINE (from IRS-DIALTECH, tel. 0689-32111) provide a similar service on safety generally, but may be less useful than TOXLINE on chemicals.

Chemical dictionaries

Chemical Synonyms and Trade Names. W. Gardner and E. Cooke. (London: Technical Press Ltd., 8th ed. 1978). The only dictionary of its kind published in the UK.

Hackh I.W.D. Chemical Dictionary. Julius Grant. (New York: McGraw Hill, 4th ed. 1969). Includes many British products.

The Condensed Chemical Dictionary. G. G. Hawley. (New York: Van Nostrand Reinhold, 8th ed. 1971). Includes many British products.

Concise Chemical and Technical Dictionary. H. Bennett. (London: Edward Arnold Ltd., 3rd ed. 1974). An American book issued by a British publisher.

Handbook of Commercial Organic Chemicals. Synthetic Organic Chemical Manufacturers' Association. American Chemical Society (1966). Mainly American products, but includes an unusual section with a breakdown of trade-name products containing mixtures of chemicals.

Merck Index. An Encyclopaedia of Chemicals and Drugs. (New Jersey: Merck Co. Inc. 9th ed. 1976). Includes many British products.

Pharmacological and Chemical Synonyms. E. E. J. Marler. (Amsterdam: Excerpta Medica, 5th ed. 1973). Deals mainly with drugs but some information on other chemicals.

Chemical formularies

These are books which give typical formulae for various kinds of products. An extract from one is shown on page 18. They won't tell you what is in a particular brand of, say, paint – but they will give you a standard formula telling you the typical composition of a paint of that kind.

The Chemical Formulary. H. Bennett (editor) (London, George Godwin Ltd., £275 for 22 volume set). More than 100,000 formulae covering adhesives, coatings, cosmetics, detergents and disinfectants, drugs, emulsions, metal treatments, polish, resins, waxes, etc.

Formulary of Paints and other Coatings. Michael and Irene Ash. (London, George Godwin Ltd., 1978, £15).

Formulary of Detergents and other Cleaning Agents. Michael and Irene Ash. (London, George Godwin Ltd, 1980, about £20).

Clinical Toxicology of Commercial Products. R. E. Gosselin and others. (Baltimore, Williams and Wilkins, 4th ed. 1976, $54.00). Contains a chapter showing typical formulae of common products pointing out in each case which of the ingredients is most likely to be dangerous.

Trade directories and technical books

General

Trade Directories of the World. (S.R.I. Ltd, 1972). A guide that will help you locate any trade directories not included in the list below.

Aerosols

Aerosol Review. (London: Morgan Grampian). Sixty-five pages of the brand names of aerosol products listing the ingredients and type of propellant.

Adhesives

Adhesives Directory. (Richmond, Surrey: A. S. O'Connor and Co. Ltd).

Adhesives Guide. B. A. Philpott. *Design Engineering* (1968).

Adhesives Handbook. J. Shields. (London: Newnes-Butterworths, 2nd ed. 1976). Some full chemical descriptions.

Chemicals and chemical industry
Chemicals 80. (London: Chemical Industries Association, 1980).
Chemical Industry Directory. (Tonbridge: Benn Brothers Ltd).
European Chemical Buyers Guide. (London: IPC Business Press).

Detergents
Domestic and Industrial Chemical Specialities. L. Chalmers.
   (London: Leonard Hill Ltd, 1966). Appendix 2 contains a full
   chemical description of trade products used in the
   manufacture of detergents and soaps.
McCutcheon's Functional Materials. (Glen Rock, USA:
   McCutcheon Publishing Co.). Mainly US products.

Finishing products
Finishing Handbook and Directory. (London: Sawell
   Publications Ltd). UK products used in the metal, wood and
   plastics finishing industries.

Paints
Paint Trade Manual of Raw Materials and Plant. (London:
   Sawell Publications Ltd). Full chemical description of
   products given in 'Resin Tables'.
Polymers, Paint and Colour Yearbook. (Redhill: Fuel and
   Metallurgical Journals Ltd).

Pesticides
British Agrochemicals Association Directory. (London: British
   Agrochemicals Association). Full chemical description of
   trade-named pesticides.
*Nanogen Index. A Dictionary of Pesticides and Chemical
   Pollutants.* Compiled by Kingsley Packer. (Updated yearly).
   (California, USA: Nanogen International Co.). Full chemical
   description of trade-named pesticides.
Pesticides Handbook – Entoma. Donald H. Frear. (Pennsylvania
   State College, USA: College Science Publishers). Full
   chemical description of trade-named pesticides.
Pesticide Manual. H. Martin and C. R. Worthing. The British
   Crop Protection Council, 4th edition 1977). Full chemical
   description of trade-named products and a summary of their
   toxic hazards.

Plastics industry

British Plastics Yearbook. (London: IPC Business Press).

European Plastics. (Holland: Economic Documentation Office).

European Plastics Buyers Guide. (London: IPC Business Press).

Laminated Plastics. D. J. Duffin. (New York: Reinhold Publishing Corp.). Products used in the US, but includes some made by British manufacturers.

Modern Plastics Encyclopaedia. (New York: McGraw Hill). Mainly US trade-named products; may include some made by British manufacturers.

Plasticisers Guidebook and Directory. (New Jersey: Noyes Data Corporation, 1972). Guide to US manufacturers with a full chemical description of trade-name products.

Polymer Additives: Guidebook and Directory. (New Jersey: Noyes Data Corporation, 1972). Guide to US manufacturers with a full chemical description of trade-name products.

Rubber industry

British Compounding Ingredients for Rubber. B. J. Wilson (Cambridge: W. Heffer and Sons Ltd, 1964). Full chemical description of 2000 trade-name products produced by British or Commonwealth manufacturers.

New Trade Names in the Rubber and Plastic Industries. (Shrewsbury: Rubber and Plastics Research Association). An annual publication which lists new trade names but gives very little information about their chemical composition.

Rubber Chemicals. C. M. van Turnhout. (Dordrecht, Holland: D. Reidel Publishing Company). A full chemical description of trade-name products, including those manufactured in the UK.

Manual for the Rubber Industry. (S. Koch, Farbenfabriken Bayer AG, 1970). Gives the full chemical description of trade-name products manufactured by Bayer.

Materials and Compounding Ingredients for Rubber. J. V. Del Gatto. (New York: Rubber World Magazine). Full chemical description of trade-name products manufactured by US companies.

Solvents

Handbook of Analysis of Organic Solvents. V. Sedivec and J. Flek. (Chichester: Ellis Horwood Ltd, 1976). Full chemical description of trade-name products given in Appendix 3.

Solvents. Thomas H. Durrans. (London: Chapman and Hall Ltd, 8th ed. 1971). Full chemical description of trade-name products in Appendix 1.

Your rights under the Health and Safety at Work Act (HSWA)

1. Duty of manufacturers

'It shall be the duty of any person who undertakes the manufacture of any substance for use at work to carry out or arrange for the carrying out of any necessary research with a view to the discovery and, so far as is reasonably practicable, the elimination or minimisation of any risks to health or safety to which the substance may give rise.'

HSWA Section 6(5)

2. Duty of manufacturers, importers or suppliers

'It shall be the duty of any person who manufactures, imports or supplies any substance for use at work . . . to take such steps as are necessary to secure that there will be available in connection with the use of the substance at work adequate information about the results of any relevant tests which have been carried out on or in connection with the substance and about any conditions necessary to ensure that it will be safe and without risks to health when properly used.'

HSWA Section 6(4) (c)

3. Duty of employers

The employer's duty includes: 'the provision of such information, instruction, training and supervision as is necessary to ensure, so far as is reasonably practicable, the health and safety at work of his employees.'

HSWA Section 2(2) (c)

4. Duty of employers to safety representatives

'The Regulations require employers to make information within their knowledge available to safety representatives necessary to enable them to fulfil their functions. Such information should include . . . information of a technical nature about hazards to health and safety and precautions deemed necessary to eliminate or minimise them in respect of machinery, plant, equipment, processes, systems of work and substances in use at work, including any relevant information provided by consultants or designers or by the manufacturer, importer or supplier of any article or substance used, or proposed to be used, at work by their employees.'

Code of Practice on Safety Representatives
approved by the Health and Safety Commission

5. Duty of factory inspectors

'. . . an inspector shall, in circumstances in which it is necessary to do so for the purpose of assisting in keeping persons (or the representatives of persons) employed at any premises adequately informed about matters affecting their health, safety and welfare, give to such persons or their representatives the following descriptions of information, that is to say –

(a) factual information obtained by him as mentioned in that subsection which relates to those premises or anything which was or is therein or was or is being done therein; and

(b) information with respect to any action which he has taken or proposes to take in or in connection with those premises in the performance of his function;

and, where an inspector does as aforesaid, he shall give the like information to the employer of the first-mentioned persons.'

HSWA Section 28(8)

The Health and Safety Commission's Advice to Suppliers

The following extracts are taken from HSC Guidance Note GS/8 'Articles and Substances for Use at Work'.

'Responsibilities concerning adequate information

51 Manufacturers, importers and suppliers of substances for use at work have a duty to ensure that adequate information about the substances they supply will be available to the user. The user, under Section 2 of the Act, has a duty to ensure the health and safety at work of his employees. To do so, he will require information about the precautions he must take with substances his employees will use. *The exact nature of the information to be available will depend on the properties of the particular substance and it is for the manufacturer, importer or supplier to satisfy himself, if necessary in consultation with the user, that the information will be adequate* (i.e. in all circumstances will be as adequate as can be reasonably expected). It is then for the user management to comply with the requirements of subsection 2(2) (c) in seeing that the ultimate user on the shop floor is provided with such information, instruction, training and supervision as is necessary to ensure, so far as is reasonably practicable, his health and safety. (subsection 6(4) (c))

"secure that there will be available"
52 In using this phrase the Section intends that the user should have ready and rapid access to the information. This does not mean that every substance supplied for use at work should be accompanied by information, but whenever a manufacturer, importer or supplier supplies a substance to a user, he should satisfy himself that he has taken the necessary steps to secure that the information is available. One method of ensuring this would be to provide the information directly with the substance. If however, the manufacturer is constantly supplying the same substance to a user, it might only be necessary to take this action on the first occasion (but see para 59).

53 A label may carry some primary warnings and instructions but, as subsequent paragraphs indicate, it will usually be necessary for more information than could readily fit onto a label to be available. The use of a data sheet could overcome this problem. Data sheets should not be regarded as precluding the use of labels; the two should be seen as complementary in appropriate cases. It may be appropriate to consider a reference to data published through other sources, e.g. the Health and Safety Executive, for instance, recommended Threshold Limit Values (TLVs), and Guidance Notes. Manufacturers, suppliers and importers should also consider other legislation affecting labelling requirements.

"adequate information"
54 In deciding how much information should be available, manufacturers, importers and suppliers should aim to strike a balance between the provision of excessive and of inadequate information. *However it is not sufficient merely to draw the attention of the user to the dangerous nature of a substance. Reference should also be made to the specific nature of the hazards and the best means of reducing or removing them.* Information should also be available in order that the user may use the substance safely. If the information is not sufficient the safety or health of those using the substance may be endangered. Manufacturers, etc. should attempt to present the information clearly and precisely and avoid the provision of excessive information which may lead to the essential facts becoming obscured.

55 The manufacturer, importer or supplier of a substance for use at work cannot always predict all the uses to which the substance may be put. Furthermore, the manufacturer cannot alter the properties of a substance so as to reduce or remove their hazardous nature. Such properties are inherent and the risks to the user may be reduced or removed by the avoidance of those conditions which accentuate or enhance them and by the adoption of proper techniques for storage, handling and use.

56 The manufacturer, etc. therefore has few opportunities, other than through the provision of information, to reduce the likelihood of the substance endangering safety and health when used at work. *He will therefore wish to ensure that the user is aware of the risks to which the substance may give rise, the circumstances in which such risks may be accentuated and the means whereby they may be reduced to a level which does not jeopardise the safety and health of the user's employees.*

"results of any relevant tests"

57 As the manufacturer, importer or supplier cannot always arrange for the availability of information to suit every individual use to which the substance may be put, the information should inform the user of the substance's properties and hazards in order than he can then decide what precautions must be taken bearing in mind the use to which the substances will be put. The Act recognises this problem in the use of the phrase "results of any relevant tests", instead of, as in subsection 6(1) (c) referring to articles (see para 31) "use for which it is designed". The information should be appropriate to the substance and should include details of such properties as flammability, explosibility, degree of toxicity, etc. Reference should also be made to any necessary recommendations for first-aid treatment to be administered in the event of unwarranted exposure, the means of controlling any outbreak of fire, etc. The user may then relate this information to his own specific needs.

"any conditions necessary"

58 In using the phrase "any conditions necessary" in subsection 6(4) (c) it is intended that the user should have available not only information about the nature of the substance but also details about the means, whereby any hazards that research or experience have indicated may arise, should be avoided. This may include *recommended handling procedures, steps to take in the event of a spillage or fire, conditions of use that should be specifically avoided* and any other particular precautions which must be taken because of the intrinsic properties of the substance.

Commitment to make further information available

59 In addition, the manufacturers, importers and suppliers of substances cannot regard the initial availability of information as necessarily constituting a complete discharge of their responsibilities under this Section. There is an implicit *commitment to remain aware of research and progress in the relevant fields and, if necessary, to ensure that up-to-date information is available* and that if any significant new information comes to light, steps should be taken to bring it to the attention of the user.'

(italics added)

Index